T0272374

SOURCE BOOKS IN ARCHITECTURE
JOHNSTON MARKLEE

SOURCE BOOKS IN ARCHITECTURE | KNOWLTON SCHOOL | THE OHIO STATE UNIVERSITY | BENJAMIN WILKE, SERIES EDITOR

15 JOHNSTON MARKLEE

|ā| | |
|ɪ:| |
|+ cl|
APPLIED
RESEARCH
+DESIGN
PUBLISHING

Published by Applied Research and Design Publishing, an imprint of ORO Editions.
Gordon Goff: Publisher

www.appliedresearchanddesign.com
info@appliedresearchanddesign.com

Copyright © 2022 Knowlton School, The Ohio State University.

All rights reserved. No part of this book may be reproduced, stored in a retrieval
system, or transmitted in any form or by any means, including electronic, mechanical,
photocopying of microfilming, recording, or otherwise (except that copying permitted by
Sections 107 and 108 of the US Copyright Law and except by reviewers for the public
press) without written permission from the publisher.

You must not circulate this book in any other binding or cover and you must impose this
same condition on any acquirer.

Contributors: Sharon Johnston, Mark Lee, Ashley Bigham, Todd Gannon, Benjamin Wilke
Book Design: Benjamin Wilke
Editor: Benjamin Wilke
Project Manager: Jake Anderson

10 9 8 7 6 5 4 3 2 1 First Edition

ISBN: 978-1-957183-25-1

Color Separations and Printing: ORO Group Inc.
Printed in Hong Kong.

AR+D Publishing makes a continuous effort to minimize the overall carbon footprint of
its publications. As part of this goal, AR+D, in association with Global ReLeaf, arranges
to plant trees to replace those used in the manufacturing of the paper produced for its
books. Global ReLeaf is an international campaign run by American Forests, one of the
world's oldest nonprofit conservation organizations. Global ReLeaf is American Forests'
education and action program that helps individuals, organizations, agencies, and
corporations improve the local and global environment by planting and caring for trees.

CONTENTS

Vault House

Pavilion of Six Views

Poggio Golo Winery

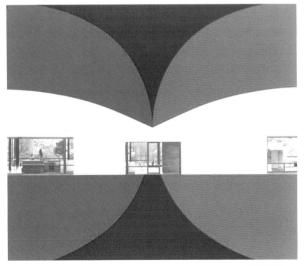

Butterfly House

UIC Center for the Arts

INTRODUCTION

BENJAMIN WILKE

I found the work of Johnston Marklee odd at first. I couldn't identify a consistent or recognizable signature. There was some repetition to motifs and forms, but the work felt too flexible and varied to signal a constant disciplinary project. Of course, I was comparing Johnston Marklee to other architects in this publication series, most of whom have a manner of form-making or representation—or some other *sine qua non*—that marks an identity that has formed, maintained, and shifted. I couldn't find the constant that provided a path to understanding this particular body of work.

But there was one thing that was consistent: the collages. Every Johnston Marklee project has a collage that provides shorthand representation of that project and that uses strategies of both *nothing* and *everything* to do its job. The *nothing* is the white silhouette that remains among the contextual queues and contexts that define it. A consistent graphic device across all of the collages, this blankness that marks the presence of the project is devoid of resolution or detail except for what the silhouette itself gives away. At the same time, the collages aim to explain *everything* about each project by distilling a set of ideas into a singular image that acts as a de facto album cover or thesis statement for the project. This strategy produces an identifying profile and a blank slate. It presents agenda and possibility. It is explicit and vague. There is the thing itself and the relationships that make it so. The collages were my way into the work of Johnston Marklee.

Once I was able to get in via an understanding of the collages, the work opened up. As the collages suggest, these aren't projects that exist as objects without context. These are not opportunities to flex an interoffice or discipline-exclusive dialogue. The projects are the medium between conditions inside and out in very conscious and considerate ways. Forms and devices often remain relatively primitive in their geometric manifestation because complexity, when warranted, arrives by way of repetition or modulation of the thing or of the qualities possessed by that thing. Dimension, scale, color, number of instances, manner of quotation, and order of arrangement are some of the ways that the same form or device can repeat, either within a single project or from one project to the next. This is one of the calling cards of the work: the use of repetition to create collections of like conditions.

Another identifiable trait of the work is a deliberate restraint on the use of forms or devices. The collages always use a limited and simple series of tools in the service of a unified aesthetic. The projects limit themselves in the number of forms used in order to explore the variables and potentials within that form. It makes sense to hear Sharon Johnston and Mark Lee talk about how they see their work, on some level, as categorizable based on the strategies used to arrange things. Understanding the projects as the result of compaction, hinging, stacking, or spanning implies the manipulation of multiples that are related by being compressed (compaction), adjacent (hinging), above or below (stacking), or extended (spanning). There are architectural mechanisms that, by their very nature, organize or collect different elements and it's no accident that these show up as prominent tools in the work of Johnston Marklee. Roofs organize a collection of things beneath them. Walls separate a collection of things on either side of them. Frames collect or isolate things within them. These organizing agents allow for the expression of both the individual elements and the collection as a whole to be legible. This is one way in which I now read the work: look for the element that repeats and look for the larger thing or mechanism that collects and organizes.

Of course, this manner of understanding the work doesn't account for the fact that projects addressed within a studio are the result of a larger team inquiry and that there are various cadences of development along the way. As this publication is merely weeks from being sent to the publisher in the spring of 2022, there has been a recent and very public reckoning with old hierarchies and labor practices that have existed as norms in architecture for too long. It feels a bit prescient for the discussion here (from November 2019) to include the topics of work-life balance and cultivating relationships both within and outside of the office. It is critical to understand that this work is not just disciplinary output framed within the context of architecture and adjacent disciplines, but also an effort by a team to address conditions out in the world with—as Sharon Johnston says here—a sense of generosity.

SHAPE AND SERIALITY

TODD GANNON

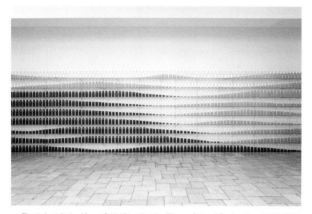

Fig. 1 Installation View, 'Critial Mass' at the Tijuana Cultural Center, Nov 10-30, 1996

Fig. 2 Palos Verdes Art Center

10 Nov 2006

I board the Pacific Surfliner at Union Station, southbound for San Diego. It's midafternoon and, though I know I'm going to roast, I slide into a window seat on the righthand side. After about an hour of nondescript warehouses and sleepy OC suburbs we trace a wide arc at Dana Point and I claim the reward for my now sun-seared brow. The Pacific opens alongside in all its horizontal splendor and for the rest of the trip I stare down at the waves that lap at the beach in slow syncopation with the clatter of the train.

I disembark at dusk and hop the tram to San Ysidro, where I walk across the border into Mexico. Fifteen minutes later the taxi deposits me at the Instituto de Cultura de Baja California. I am maybe an hour early for the opening of *Critical Mass* [**Fig. 1**], an installation by Johnston Marklee (JML), the Los Angeles-based architecture firm led by Sharon Johnston and Mark Lee.

Inside, eight glass shelves on metal standards line two walls of the gallery. The shelves support several hundred identical glass bottles arranged in neat rows, with a ninth row placed on the floor beneath the lowest shelf. The bottles have been filled to varying levels with apple-colored liquids to suggest attenuated waves across the array. Gala gives way to Granny Smith as the eye travels bottom to top and left to right. I am informed that the height of the liquid indexes the population of residents living in irregular and planned housing settlements in Tijuana, but this seems less the point of the exhibition than a kind of ruse, extraneous trivia deployed primarily to justify continued staring at the glistening *ondas de colores*.

So, I stare. Before long, red bottles appear to advance in my field of vision as green ones recede, an effect that renders the ensemble an illusory seascape, islands on a placid sea. Oblique views, especially from the corner of one's eye, highlight the shimmer of the glass, which makes the waves seem to move. After three hours on the train, the ABBA spacing of the standards against the even staccato of the bottles does not seem the least bit accidental.

The show was mesmerizing. But it seemed to have less to do with JML's then-current concerns than with preoccupations I thought they had left behind. At the time, the firm was enjoying the groundswell of attention that erupted upon completion of the Hill House in Pacific Palisades. This justly celebrated work marked a significant swerve for the still-young office, one that appeared to move away from themes of seriality and repetition that drove earlier projects toward a pursuit of arresting singular shapes.

Consider the Palos Verdes Art Center competition entry of 2000, an important early effort and crucial ancestor of *Critical Mass*. Here, JML unifies an elegantly rambling collection of low volumes by floating a vast abstracted pergola overhead [**Fig. 2**]. Fashioned of translucent acrylic in an otherwise basswood model, the canopy is rectilinear in plan, though each of its vertical fins is shaped with gentle curves top and bottom that render the array a single, rippling surface. In some photos the project seems to prefigure the installation in Tijuana, with the horizontal array flattening to the vertical picture plane. In others it calls to mind more distant affiliations including the Shroud of Turin, a ghostly surface that similarly suggests a corporeality that is no longer—or perhaps never was—present.

Fig. 3 Orchid Restaurant

Though JML's scheme for Palos Verdes went unrealized, the firm completed a version of its sculpted canopy at the Penner House in Palm Springs in 2000. Not long after, they returned to the undulating overhead plane in the Orchid restaurant in Santa Monica [**Fig. 3**]. Reversing the approach in Palos Verdes, where they conjure a virtual surface from an abundance of structure, here an actual surface floats above with no indication of support. Yet seriality remains in the unashamedly visible panel joints, which register the ceiling's reticulation as they trace undulated curves across its luminous topography.

Fig. 4 Sale House and 2-4-6-8 House beyond

By then, Johnston Marklee had already completed an important early commission in which repetition reappears in a new, stealthier form. The Sale House [**Fig. 4**] replaces a Venice bungalow on the same property as the 2-4-6-8 House by Morphosis. A key early work by the firm then led by Thom Mayne and Michael Rotondi, 2-4-6-8 comprises a 20-foot square studio volume, clad in asphalt shingles and capped with a pyramidal metal roof, perched atop a two-car garage of colored concrete block [**Fig. 5**]. On each wall of the studio the architects locate a single foursquare window, each one incrementally larger than its neighbor to the left. Turn in circles at the center of the space and the windows will appear to expand and contract as you spin.

Taking their cues from the earlier structure, JML repeats the square plan of 2-4-6-8's upper volume twice—first to form the main volume of the new house and again to define the central void of its patio. Each of the four original windows is echoed in the upper part of the new house, though here they align at the head rather than the sill and are displaced to the edge of each facade.[1] The displacement of the upper windows occurs in the opposite direction of their increase in size (which itself reverses 2-4-6-8's clockwise expansion), a move that both reinforces and counters

Fig. 5 2-4-6-8 House

Fig. 6 Hill House

Fig. 7 View Houe

the centrifugal force implied by the earlier work and sets up the diagonal vistas that slice through the otherwise orthogonal plan. Importantly, JML adds a section of brake metal to turn the corner at each of the four windows. These crucial additions subtly reprise (and relocate) the bright blue transoms and red rain deflectors that cap Morphosis's foursquare openings as they signal the rotational energy of the interior spaces. In yet another reversal, JML relocates 2-4-6-8's iconic colors to the interior, answering the white box of Morphosis's studio with spaces saturated in chromatic variations on the original's primary exterior palette.[2]

For all this cat-and-mouse formal play (and there is plenty more where this came from), the breakthrough at the Sale House comes in the calculated awkwardness of its exterior massing and fenestration. This quality, hilariously captured in a cheeky photo-essay-cum-comic-strip by Walead Beshty,[3] is even more pronounced at the Hill House [**Fig. 6**], with its leering jack-o-lantern facade, and the View House [**Fig. 7**], with its unsettling top-heavy massing. From around 2002, the development of carefully calibrated awkwardness appears to eclipse repetition—and the formal elegance they routinely derived from it—as JML's central preoccupation.

In his excellent little book, *Awkwardness*, theologian and cultural critic Adam Kotsko explores the redemptive socio-political possibilities of this pervasive condition.[4] Etymologically "going the wrong way," awkwardness is what happens when social norms break down. Think of the clumsy elbow-bumping that replaced handshakes during the COVID-19 pandemic or the confused stammering that often accompanies the adoption of gender-neutral pronouns. In Kotsko's view, awkwardness is everywhere. But rather than see it as a problem, he finds in it a powerful motivator to invent new forms of social interaction that accept difference and proliferate novelty.

Though Kotsko develops his arguments in the context of contemporary film and television sitcoms, his ideas as easily could have been inspired by Johnston Marklee's architecture. Deploying something like the "radical awkwardness" Kotsko identifies in *Curb Your Enthusiasm*'s Larry David, JML does not seek to overcome awkwardness through ironic detachment, as the character Jim does in *The Office*. Nor do they use it to shore up flagging cultural institutions, as Judd Apatow uses the "bromance" as a crutch for traditional marriage in his films. Instead, JML orchestrates the new social and spatial arrangements that awkward situations demand. At the Sale House, they suggest how to play by the rules and simultaneously do your own thing—an excellent model for anyone trying to coexist with a distinguished member of another generation. At the Hill House, they take the frustrating limitations of hillside zoning as a catalyst for an inventive rearrangement of residential form and the domestic life it stages. At the View House, traditional notions of front, back, top, and bottom slacken to the point of irrelevance as JML negotiates conflicting demands to maximize floor area while minimizing footprint and to guarantee both expansive views and intimate privacy.

In each case, JML embraces an "awkward position," aiming for an architecture that is at once unashamedly incongruous and undeniably logical in response to its circumstances.[5] At its best, their work is not "so wrong it's right," but rather so comfortably both that when called upon to describe it, the adjectives "right" and "wrong" simply dissolve into meaninglessness. What remains is a compelling sense of "on-purposeness," an air of conviction with intellectual roots stretching back through the writings of Michael Fried and Horatio Greenough at least as far as those of Immanuel Kant.

At the same time, JML sidesteps the self-contained modernism Fried found in Anthony Caro's sculpture, Greenough found in sailing ships, and Kant found in rose petals.[6] Understanding that such appeals to autonomy come off today as less self-sufficient than self-righteous, JML is careful never to fully disengage purposiveness from purpose. And though their work is steeped in the history and theory of the modern movement and often directly references the architecture of the past, the firm is steadfast in its refusal to adopt historical tropes as given or rehearse modern myths as dogma. As they make clear in the exquisite photomontages they have produced over the last decade, Johnston Marklee does not appropriate historical sources. Rather, they insinuate themselves into canonical contexts [**Fig. 8**].[7]

With the Sale, Hill, and View Houses, JML established themselves as formidable talents and key purveyors of what Bob Somol refers to, in an influential riff on a concept introduced by Michael Fried, as "shape."[8] Gathering further intellectual support from Marshall McLuhan, Dave Hickey, and others, Somol proposes shape—easy, adaptable, expendable—as a potent alternative to the difficult, inflexible, self-serious contortions of form that had become prevalent in the wake of the so-called digital turn of the late 1990s. Driving his point home in McLuhanesque terms, Somol pronounces form—and the critical legacy from which it springs—too hot. Shape, on the other hand, along with the projective possibilities it signals, is just cool.[9] And in the overheated architectural scene of the mid-aughts in L.A., nobody seemed quite as cool as Johnston Marklee.

Fig. 8 Hill House

Fig. 9 Hong Kong Design Institute

So, as I rode back to Los Angeles after the opening of *Critical Mass*, I wondered what to make of JML's return to repetition, an interest which seemed only to intensify in the projects that followed. A few months later the installation made a second, smaller appearance at UCLA and, the following summer, a third at the MOCA Temporary Contemporary. This time the bottles appear as playfully inverted chandeliers in dialogue with Frank Gehry's iconic canopy above.

Though the office still pursued overtly figural work—the Hungry Cat restaurant in Hollywood, the masterful first Kauai House project—seriality continued to reappear, and to do so more and more forcefully, in unrealized projects such as those for the SCPR/KPCC Headquarters in Pasadena, the Hong Kong Design Institute, and the San Vitores Plaza in Guam. Hong Kong marks another significant breakthrough, with the repetition of simple shapes combining with an unlikely massing strategy to produce an urban streetscape and an exuberant central atrium [**Fig. 9**]. Variations on

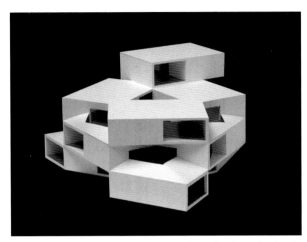

Fig. 10 Gran Traiano Arts Complex

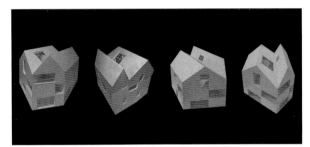

Fig. 11 House House

Flg. 12 Vault House

the theme arrived at a steady clip over the next few years, with the collection of buildings for the Gran Traiano Art Complex in Grottaferrata, Italy [**Fig. 10**], crystallizing the approach into a catalog of possibilities in which the repetition of simple cubic elements, always punctuated by oversized apertures, combines with equally simple formal operations (mostly stacking and rotation) to generate exactly the kind of arresting singular shapes JML earlier had produced by—temporarily, I now knew—setting seriality aside.

Two additional projects, both initiated in 2008, introduce crucial moves into the JML playbook. The House House in Ordos, China [**Fig. 11**], builds on the stack-and-rotate methods of Grottaferrata, but rather than seek coherence in closed geometrical matrices or impose it with subtractive sweeps, here the architects arrive at an unlikely unity by adding cartoonishly simple gables to the mix. These curious elements—absent, near as I can tell, in the firm's portfolio up to that point—come into dramatic tension with the alternating solids and voids of the bulk of the building. At the same time, the gable's repetition, as well as the canted upper story and non-orthogonal slices at each end, guarantee that the project never settles back into the iconic familiarity that gables normally imply. Instead, the House House oscillates in and out of coherence or, rather, it cycles through a series of equally convincing impressions of coherence, none of which easily resolve with another. Is this one house or many? Public or private? Solid or hollow? Everyday or alien? The answer, in each case, is yes.

The Vault House [**Fig. 12**], completed on a beachfront site in Oxnard in 2013, similarly unsettles one of architecture's most familiar elements. Here, as they had done at the Hill House, JML uses strict zoning constraints as a jumping off point. But where in the Palisades they proceed by way of clever subtractions from the allowable volume, in Oxnard they pack that volume with an assortment of vaulted spaces like loaves in a breadbox, each one tracing a different elliptical profile than its neighbor. As Somol notices in a perceptive essay, there seem to be more loaves than the box can contain—some appear to have been sliced off at the perimeter, suggesting that the matrix of spaces might well be understood to continue in every direction as a template for future development.[10]

Each vault spans crosswise, parallel to the shoreline beyond, and corresponds to an individual unit of program. Spaces within open one onto the next, which, combined with generous interior windows and a clever split-level section, affords ocean views to even the most distant rooms. In a sly reversal of the strategy at Palos Verdes, the arrangement combines two normally contrasting spatial conditions, with an open floor plan simultaneously defined, by the collection of vaults above, as a series of cellular volumes arranged in a loose, telescoping enfilade from street to beach.

On each of the long facades JML arrays a series of arched openings. These are oriented normally at the main level but upside down at the upper floor, which makes all of them read less like conventional arches than abstract figures. At times, they appear to drape from the parapet, like beach towels hung out to dry. At others, they seem like scoops removed from the thick mass of the building, making the curious voids along its base seem similarly subtractive, like misplaced lengths of cavetto molding or a massive Egyptian cornice in the process of being carved.

If, in Ordos, gables productively fail to perform a conventionally stabilizing role, the vaults in Oxnard similarly shrug off traditional associations with the support of structural loads. Throughout, they flaunt their freedom from structural responsibility, springing apparently unsupported from non-existent beams and intersecting one another with wanton disregard for conventional tectonics. At the ends of the vaulted volumes, their curved edges often capriciously change directions to join with the arched punches on the facades, unfurling graceful, Art Nouveau curves whiplike across the interior [**Fig. 13**]. These starkly contrast both the abrupt intersections of the layered vaults as well as the cartoony stubbiness of their container to suggest, as at Ordos, a surprisingly happy marriage of elegant seriality and awkward shape.

*

In the projects represented in this volume, Johnston Marklee deploy both shape and seriality with equal dexterity to conjure surprising new possibilities from conventional architectural elements. At the Porch House, [**Fig. 14**] building tectonics, typically suppressed in the JML oeuvre up to that point, take center stage. The roughly 90-foot by 30-foot block of the house is supported by a concrete frame of six equal bays and gently bowed to embrace a steep ravine in Pacific Palisades. Flaunting neighborhood norms, the architects orient the short end of the block to the street, placing what functions as the front of the house where one would expect to find the side and allowing the broad west facade to command breathtaking views across an adjacent state park to the ocean. Slipping past the bunkerlike street elevation, visitors are funneled between gentle curves along a concrete bridge cantilevered from the east face of the house. A glazed central area marks the entry and redirects

Fig. 13 Vault House living room

Fig. 14 Porch House living room

attention to the sweeping vista. Stepping inside, one senses the cunning conventionality of the plan, which reveals itself to be as unabashedly symmetrical as a Palladian villa. Below, bedrooms recover the repetitive rhythm of the concrete frame, while clever curves rehearse the entry's westward sweep toward the view. On the upper level, similar curves grant an unexpectedly figural quality to areas for work, study, and exercise.

For all this, what dominates the experience of the Porch House is JML's carefully calibrated dematerialization of its concrete construction. On the approach from the street, the architects stress the stolid mass of bearing walls, gathering heavy concrete surfaces around visitors—first at right, then left, then above—as they approach. Upon entry, the sense of mass is eclipsed by the expansive view, an effect made all the more powerful when the glass panels to the west are retracted. Though the house maintains its openness when this glazed curtain is closed,

Fig. 15 Casa de Mont double-height entry

Fig. 16 Hut House

Fig. 17 Hut House courtyard

drawing it back renders the house nothing but porch and the concrete near weightless, little more than a gentle reminder of the claustrophobic urbanity lucky visitors have left behind.

At the de Mont House [**Fig. 15**], JML again takes up the tectonics of structural frames, but here combines them with the packed interior volumes of the Vault House. Breaching the entry facade through another centrally located portal, one's eye is drawn first up and out of the house via the sculpted oculus above, and then through it to the triangular gallery and living spaces beyond. Accommodations for cooking, relaxing, sleeping, and study take their places along the curved southern edge of the building, with each opening onto a generous terrace that spans the width of the house. The simplicity of the plan belies the complexity of the spaces within, which, like the voluptuous volumes concealed behind the stately facade of a French *hôtel particulier* (cf. Antoine Le Pautre's 1657 Hôtel de Beauvais in Paris), develop unperturbed by the straightforward frame that contains them.

The Hut House in Kauai similarly harbors an unlikely complexity within a familiar form [**Figs. 16, 17**]. Here, a series of simple geometrical operations transforms a traditional Hawaiian roof into an exercise in rotational dynamics. To be sure, the compositional DNA of the Sale House is present in Kauai, but here the action is centripetal, with the pinwheeling volumes of the living spaces pulled in from the perimeter frame toward the gentle vortex of the courtyard. Once again, overhead elements—asymmetrical gables, torqued skylights, and, as if to obviate the rotational theme, quietly whirring ceiling fans—perform the organizational work typically assigned to walls. These, where they are permitted to remain, are dutifully straightforward, providing a backstop to the generous veranda from which expansive views of the surrounding landscape, framed by the marching perimeter columns, are available in every direction.

Now in its third decade, Johnston Marklee has become increasingly engaged with large-scale institutional commissions. Some, like their proposal for a Center for the Arts at the University of Illinois in Chicago [**Fig. 18**], draw directly on earlier experiments with seriality, shape, and dematerialization. Here, the stepped profile, translucent skin, scalloped surfaces, and rose-colored palette frankly recall the third iteration of *Critical Mass* at MOCA. Others, like the Miami Design District, the phase I renovation and masterplan for the Museum of Contemporary Art Chicago, and a proposal for Philadelphia Contemporary, press their investigations into new territory. In Miami, Johnston Marklee orchestrates the Porch House's dissolution of mass in elevation rather than plan, with the bulk of the building evaporating from solid to sky over three levels [**Fig. 19**]. In Philadelphia, frame aspires to figure in a playful collection of steel platforms and gable-roofed pavilions appended to a straightforward shell containing galleries, educational spaces, and administrative functions [**Fig. 20**]. In respectful homage to local legends Robert Venturi and Denise Scott Brown, whose 1979 Institute for Scientific Information headquarters sits on an adjacent site to the southeast, Johnston Marklee wrap their building in a diaphanous skin which complements the Institute's pixelated brick, append it with a supergraphic frieze reminiscent of Venturi's landmark Guild House of 1963, and present one of their gabled pavilions as a white steel frame, recalling Venturi and Scott Brown's own ghostly reconstruction of a gabled structure in Franklin Court (1976).

At 48,000 square feet, the Margo Leavin Graduate Art Studios for UCLA stands as Johnston Marklee's largest completed building to date. Located in Culver City's Hayden Tract, a neighborhood of light-industrial buildings made famous in architectural circles by Eric Owen Moss's exuberant interventions, the project more than doubles the size of an existing warehouse that has provided working space for UCLA art students since 1986. The architects begin by stripping away a collection of obsolete structures that had accreted to the warehouse and extending the raised ground plane of the remaining building to the perimeter of the site. On this new plinth, they arrange a collection of communal facilities— gallery, woodshop, ceramics studio—and three indoor-outdoor courtyards, leaving the existing building to house individual studio spaces. To bring coherence to the complex, JML again turn to serial overhead elements, repeating the vaulted forms of the original warehouse to enclose the new perimeter.

In keeping with the students' desire that the new facility maintain the workaday roughness of the original structure (and, no doubt, aiming for maximum contrast with Moss's Vespertine restaurant across the street) JML proceed with a light touch and deploy a minimum of overt Design, adopting instead a restrained, lower-case approach that stresses clarity, simplicity, and frill-free accommodation. Mechanical equipment, electrical conduit, and production machinery are left frankly exposed throughout. Existing bowstring-truss roofs are refurbished but otherwise left as found. New roofs retain the shape of the existing trusses but reimagine their tectonics, with glue-laminated timbers increasing the size while reducing the number and complexity of structural members, which allows for the inclusion of integrated skylights at each new bay and suffuses the space with an elegant abstraction. This

Fig. 18 UIC Center for the Arts

Fig. 19 Miami Design District

Fig. 20 Philadelphia Contemporary

Fig. 21 UCLA Margo Leavin Graduate Art Studios entry courtyard

Fig. 22 UCLA Margo Leavin Graduate Art Studios southwest facade

quality is particularly apparent in the open-air courtyards, which are capped with translucent PVC membranes [**Fig. 21**].

For all this, an air of calculated awkwardness remains apparent throughout. The building's stout proportions and singular roof shapes certainly contribute, but it is the architects' deliberate suppression of mid-scale articulation that guarantees the effect. From the start, Johnston Marklee has steadfastly refused to play conventional games with parts and wholes. For them, it's all whole, save for few well-placed holes. Though they often deploy repetitive elements, these are rarely broken down further and inevitably reinforce the coherence of the overall mass over the integrity of constituent components.

Such is the case with the tilt-up concrete panels that wrap the UCLA studios. Cast with serial convexities that mimic in miniature the rhythm of the roofs, the panels are otherwise unarticulated and stop several feet short of the sidewalk, with their curves bulging several inches proud of the concrete foundation. This produces a scalloped shadow (another recapitulation of the roofline) along the bottom of the panels and imparts to the heavy concrete the lightness of a curtain. At the courtyards, the panels are simply sheared off to allow interior activities to activate the street, with chain-link enclosures providing a gauzy interface between. Especially against an overcast sky, the repetitive concrete suggests an unlikely softness, like quilted padding cushioning the nascent artworks within [**Fig. 22**].

An unbuilt competition entry, the Rice University Visual & Dramatic Arts (VADA) building would replace a much loved but inadequate media center on the edge of the Rice University campus, gathering currently dispersed academic and public programs into a single building [**Fig. 23**]. Retaining the memory of the existing metal shed in the new design, JML adopts its simple gable-roofed massing and repeats it over four equal bays alongside Michael Maltzan's 2017 Moody Center for the Arts.[11] To accommodate a sizeable program without overpowering its low-slung neighbor, JML employs a stepped section to increase the height of the building incrementally from two stories to four. The three rows of gables that result register Maltzan's loose nine-square plan with each step. In keeping with the restrained historicism of the central campus, the architects arrange VADA's west front symmetrically, employ a simple grid of fenestration throughout, and present a red brick skin to the neighborhood beyond.

This apparently well-behaved contextualism recalls the reticence shown by James Stirling in his 1982 addition to the nearby Rice

School of Architecture. ("I went to Rice to see the building, but couldn't find it," Philip Johnson once joked.) And yet, as at Stirling's building, a mischievous playfulness pervades the VADA scheme. Though its formal vocabulary derives from its staid surroundings, the quirky abstraction with which it is shaped makes clear that this is anything but a rehearsal of neoclassical norms. The brick of the west front is arranged in jaunty zigzags that, like the UCLA facade, replay the roof as elevation and add textural relief to otherwise blank expanses of brick.[12] On the north elevation, JML swings open the base of the building and foregoes brick for metal siding, signaling VADA's casual intimacy with the Moody Center and revealing the cacophony of creative activity within. Approached off axis, the building's spiky crenellations appear raucously animated, like cardboard waves cut out by giants for a grade-school play.

At the Menil Drawing Institute in Houston, which adds 30,000 square feet to the suburban arts campus anchored by Renzo Piano's masterful Menil Collection building of 1987, Johnston Marklee orchestrates a symphonic integration of earlier experiments with seriality, shape, and dematerialization. In plan, the architects arrange eight 60-foot square modules in offset rows of four, placing a public gallery flanked by two open-air courtyards along a quiet residential street and nestling support functions and a third courtyard into the residential fabric to the north. As at the Sale House, the module refers to a nearby building of note, in this case Piano's Cy Twombly Pavilion (1995) to the northwest.[13] Each courtyard is capped with a curious truncated pyramid (shades of the Hut House?) which has been inverted and balanced atop thin walls to hover improbably over elegantly planted gardens. Similar roofs are perched atop the gallery and administrative spaces. Where modules meet, their sloping surfaces join to trace the familiar profile of a suburban gable. As at the Vault House, these appear to have been packed into the volume of the building and sheared off at its perimeter to suggest a continuity between interior spaces and the neighborhood beyond.

On my first visit to the Institute, a warm Saturday morning not long after it opened, the sky is so blue it seems artificial. Passing through a tidy residential neighborhood of mostly one-story bungalows, the car eases to the curb alongside the white steel panels that define the long, low volume of the building. The casual simplicity of the approach—no garage, no ticket, no institutional ceremony—reinforces the facility's deference to its suburban surroundings. In the bright sun the steel panels seem more irreal than the sky, less physical stuff than surgical excisions

Fig. 23 Rice University Visual & Dramatic Arts, with Moody Center beyond

Fig. 24 Menil Drawing Institute

of matter from the world. The effect is uncanny, and immediately calls to mind JML's iconic photomontage of the Hill House, suggesting that the image's powerful blankness is less a graphic conceit than a now-realized material ambition.

Thirty-six feet wide, the panels stand 120 feet apart and are joined at the top by a thin white line—eight inches thick, laser-straight, sixteen feet above grade—that extends twelve feet past the end of each panel and then turns the corner to join with matching panels to the east and west. [**Fig. 24**] A view from across the street reveals a strict ABA symmetry, with the blank cedar-clad block of the gallery directly on center. Set back from the steel and finished in a rich dark grey, the block tends to vanish into the void of the courtyards, leaving the panels to dominate the ensemble, a phalanx of alien figures laying claim to an unassuming patch of suburban lawn [**Fig. 25**].

Fig. 25 Menil Drawing Institute west entry courtyard and south porch

A gabled void signals access to the entry courtyard [**Fig. 26**]. Here, the annular arrangement, serene planting, and apparently weightless roofs encourage monastic contemplation, while the gables suggest the loose informality of the neighborhood. Throughout, the building oscillates between these two impressions. Cerebral cloister or everyday abode? Familiar forms or incongruous shapes? Casual continuity or awkward interruption? As at the House House, the answer is always yes.

Within, a central "living room" joins the gallery block to the band of support functions to the north. Overhead, a gabled ceiling dances in expressionistic folds that, upon inspection, resolve into familiar ridges, valleys, and dormers [**Fig. 27**]. Despite its name, the overriding impression of the space is less living room than elegantly abstracted attic. What better place to discover and contemplate precious drawings? And yet, the room's relative brightness and meticulous craft signal that JML has perpetrated yet another cunning conversion of the commonplace. Surveying the scene, one quickly realizes there are no drawings on display. These can be found, shielded from the living room's damaging light levels, in the adjacent gallery. Here, as my eyes adjust to the subdued illumination, the genius of JML's method snaps vividly into focus. Unsatisfied merely to borrow the lively geometries of the suburban attic to animate their architecture, the architects have imported the attic's distinctive quality of light as well! Then, in a virtuoso feat of architectural transfiguration, they detach that familiar atmosphere from the forms that produce it, displacing the attic's dimness to the

gallery beyond. Stripped of persistent shadows and shorn of fussy stick-frame articulations, the attic forms now exude the conviction of singular shapes that, when serialized across the matrix of its ceilings, make the Menil a tour de force of awkward elegance and Johnston Marklee's most impressive institutional building to date.

NOTES

1 The garage door reappears as well, in the proportionally similar glass that defines the living room.

2 The color scheme is a product of a collaboration between Johnston Marklee and the artist Jeff Elrod.

3 Walead Beshty, "…," in Reto Geiser, ed., *House Is a House Is a House Is a House Is a House: Architectures and Collaborations of Johnston Marklee* (Basel: Birkhäuser, 2016): 161–76.

4 Adam Kotsko, *Awkwardness* (Winchester, UK: Zero Books, 2010).

5 Cf. Andrew Zago, "Awkward Position," *Perspecta 42* (2010): 209–22.

6 See Michael Fried, "Art and Objecthood," *Artforum 5* (June 1967): 12–23; Horatio Greenough, "American Architecture" (1843), in *Form and Function: Remarks on Art, Design, and Architecture* (Berkeley: University of California Press, 1947): 51–68; and Immanuel Kant, *Critique of Judgment* (New York: Hafner Press, [1790] 1951).

7 In lieu of further comment on these extremely intelligent images, I refer readers to Stan Allen's excellent analysis in "Folding Time: Johnston Marklee's Plural Temporalities," *El Croquis 198* (2019): 258–275.

8 R.E. Somol, "Twelve Reasons to Get Back into Shape," in Rem Koolhaas, *Content* (Köln: Taschen, 2004): 86–87. For Fried's postulation of shape, see "Shape as Form: Frank Stella's New Paintings," *Artforum 5* (Nov 1966): 18–27.

9 On the critical/projective dyad, see R.E. Somol and Sarah Whiting, "Notes on the Doppler Effect and Other Moods of Modernism," *Perspecta 33* (2002): 72–77.

10 R.E. Somol, "Grind Houses," *2G* 67 (2013): 12.

11 JML previously experimented with serialized gable-roofed sheds for the Green Line Arts Center in Chicago and the Beverly Hills Art Shed, completed in 2016.

12 Those familiar with the Rice campus will sense in this chamfered facade a subtle nod to John Outram's riotously postmodern Duncan Hall (1996), just off the main quad.

13 To better calibrate their building to the scale of the neighborhood, JML borrows just a foursquare corner from Piano's nine-square plan. Across a broad lawn to the west, they repeat the full 90-foot square block to house an energy building for the Menil campus.

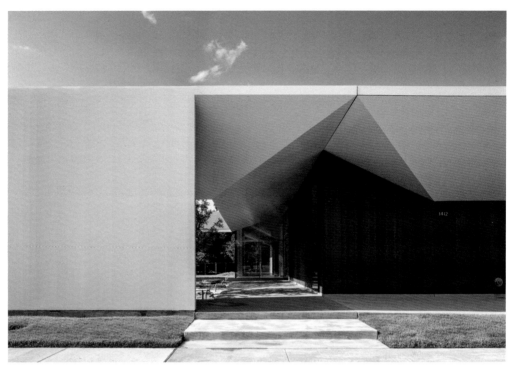

Fig. 26 Menil Drawing Institute south elevation detail

Fig. 27 Living room, looking to scholar courtyard and entry

A DISCUSSION WITH SHARON JOHNSTON AND MARK LEE

The following conversation between Ashley Bigham, Sharon Johnston, Mark Lee, and students of the Knowlton School was recorded during the 2019-2020 school year at The Ohio State University. It has been edited for clarity.

SHARON JOHNSTON: Thank you for having us. The first collection of buildings we're going to discuss are smaller buildings, mostly houses. All of them have a particular issue that drove the project. Later on, we will discuss projects where the objects begin to multiply. For these conversations, we've categorized our work according to a number of themes that are fairly consistent: *compaction*, *hinging and stacking*, and *spanning*. There's certainly an evolution to these categories, but they all have to do with approaches to scale and program. There's almost a proto-urbanism to the projects, whether they're literally in a more urban setting or not. Part of the multiplication that happens—and one of the ways in which we think about objects—is to understand even singular objects as made up of multiple things; it's very foundational and primitive in some ways. Spanning coincides with the larger buildings that come into play as our practice has evolved and where you start to see the roof structure as something that begins to organize a collection of what are essentially small buildings within the domain of the roof. The frame is something that we're exploring a bit more in our work right now. It implies a certain kind of porosity in projects that we're working on currently, whether it's a house or an institutional project. Framing is more expressive as opposed to being embodied within the object or being inside of a building. It's a condition that is almost conceived like infrastructure, where it's really more of a frame or platform and the program is much more flexible in the way that it occupies that ground. So that's a general context for the work we're going to show and the relationship of these projects to the projects we're working on now.

MARK LEE: I think this has been a nice opportunity for us to organize the projects in some interdisciplinary manner, because the projects oftentimes deal with so many other contingencies that involve such a wide range of concerns: climate change, migration, social housing, and so on. I think that once in a while it's good for architecture to retreat from this and to just focus on its respective formation, symbiosis, and such. So that's how we've organized this; it's going to be presented much more one-dimensionally than it actually is.

I think there are architects who establish a disciplinary project very early on in their career. Then there are architects who work very specifically with site or context and over time they'll cultivate or discover a certain disciplinary project. And then there are architects who will never have a specific disciplinary project. We're definitely not the first kind. We'll let you decide if we're the second or third kind. So why don't we start?

The Sale House is in Venice, California. The main building was attached to an early Morphosis project, the 2-4-6-8 House. The main house burned down in a fire and the same client commissioned us to redo it such that it would be attached to the 2-4-6-8 House. We started off looking at a number of these California school Venice projects and we really liked the idea of our building as a background so as not to get into any kind of contest with the 2-4-6-8 House.

The organization is very simple. We had about 1600 square feet to work with; it's a relatively small project. We knew we wanted a courtyard, so we took the dimensions of the 2-4-6-8 House—which is 20 feet by 20 feet—and we created a courtyard that's 20 feet by 20 feet. The master suite above is also 20 feet by 20 feet. We repeated the mass and took the same dimensions and, rather than centering any windows, we pushed the windows to the edges of the mass.

We began to think about color and invited the artist Jeff Elrod to collaborate. He was a young artist at the time. Instead of the primary colors of red, yellow, and blue in Morphosis's project, you find cyan, magenta, and yellow for our interior. So we've altered and internalized the color from the Morphosis project. This happens in the rooms that are not the primary living spaces that you spend the most time in. It happens in the bedrooms, bathrooms, or stairwell that are more transitional spaces. The exterior color is a gray tone from a photographic gray card, which is a calibrating tool for use with analog cameras. It defines the most neutral color that brings out the highest saturation of other colors, so the exterior is meant to be as neutral as it can be. It's a very modestly-budgeted project, so we try to focus on where the design energy and contrast could be. It's a simple stucco building, and we have fairly standard windows, but the first of the key details happens when the windows are pushed to the edge. A number of small but significant details are required to keep these windows at the edge and to allow the alignment of certain edges and volumes where we want them. It's not super visible to the naked eye, but more standardized construction would try to avoid such things.

For us, this makes something enigmatic out of a very simple bottle of space. There's no question that we're looking at Venturi and how flatness exists in contrast with something that's very deep. There's a flatness that's reinforced by the frame and that is pushed out like a volume in the lower part of the house, versus the frames that are flush and pushed to the edge in the upper volume.

I don't want to make a huge deal out of this small house, but it's an important moment—not so much in terms of the language, but in terms of the planning. It's a pretty standard house for the area size-wise, but it has outdoor spaces like the courtyard and the roof deck that promote interactions with the outside. This comes up again and again later on in our work.

When you're in the main spaces, you don't directly see the color on the walls upstairs, but you see the reflection of that color in these shared, white spaces, whether during daytime or at night. So these are spaces that are shaped and compacted because we want to arrange so many of them next to this 20 x 20 x 20 space. This is an early instance of the what we refer to as compaction.

JOHNSTON: The Sale House was the first time that we had a deep engagement with an existing building as part of an historic continuum and dialogue. This is also when we started working with artists on our projects. This certainly had a lot to do with color, but it included dialogue about the project as it evolved, formally and otherwise.

STUDENT: Can you say what the budget was?

LEE: It was about $250 per square-foot.

STUDENT: What kind of limitations did you have to set? Formal organization? Details? Materials?

LEE: We considered many options. We knew that if we spread out the design focus evenly with respect to the budget, it would look like a stucco box. It still does in a way, but in a slightly enig-

Sale House, northwest corner

matic manner. So, we decided to focus on where we could be more transgressive.

JOHNSTON: Generally-speaking, it's a wood frame building and that's the cheapest way you can build in L.A. But some of the window offsets required the introduction of steel. As Mark said, it's not about evenly distributing our budget, but instead about focusing energy in certain places. I think it's important that it doesn't scream out at you that, oh, this was the expensive part of the building. It becomes part of a holistic approach. Things like the courtyard and having a void or making an open room...those were moves that we made that allow the house to approximate something bigger because of the extended views they create while keeping the footprint small.

LEE: In terms of budget distribution, with real estate like this—a $250 per square-foot building—the contractor is going to tell you that you can afford this type of window with this type of hardware and this type of detail. And no matter how talented you are as an architect, in the end it will look like a $250 per square-foot building. To turn it from a building into architecture, you need a dynamic distribution of both the budget and the design energy. Great architects know how to do that. In other words, you have maybe 10% of the building where you spend a thousand dollars per square foot and the rest of the building is $200 per square-foot. I think the difference for us is that the areas where we spent a thousand dollars per square foot are not the ones that are noticeable right away. It's a little bit more invisible for us. We don't necessarily feel the need to show you where we spent the money. It can be a little bit more backgrounded and I think that's okay.

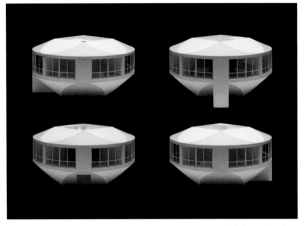

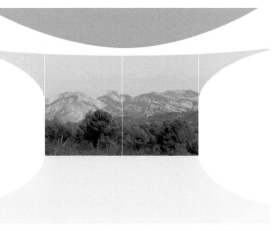

Solo House elevations

Solo House collage

ASHLEY BIGHAM: It's interesting to think that this was one of your early projects and that, since paint is relatively inexpensive, you paint the walls in a very particular way. It seems like a great way to get something that is architectural and high quality, but for a somewhat modest cost.

LEE: Absolutely. I think it's also about looking at how artists respond to a visual problem. There's always a lesson in seeing how a collaborator from another field will look at a problem differently. We probably wouldn't have thought to use a photographic gray card. We probably would have picked another color. Maybe we'd find the more normal things that are happening with the other neighborhood houses and make that part of the context. Working with Jeff Elrod here really reinforced an understanding of the value of collaborations like this, and how they quite literally import other forms of expertise and awareness into a project. We find real value in that.

With the Solo House, we had a slightly different starting point. This project is an unbuilt proposal for a house in Spain between Barcelona and Valencia; it's situated in the hills in a really beautiful landscape. The developer brought in 20 or so architects to each design a house, all of which are quite isolated from one another. Our site is on very flat terrain in the middle of an elm grove. With elm trees, the foliage spreads horizontally; these trees don't get very tall.

So there's a panoramic landscape and our first instinct was to design a round building that's raised. We thought it would be really beautiful to sit atop the elm canopy, especially when the leaves are in bloom. In terms of divisions for rooms, there was a general

desire to have a series of bedrooms and living spaces, but we also imagined a single person or couple occupying the house, where this kind of division may not be necessary. We began to consider the possibility of all the doors sliding open so that one could walk around the entire house. It's a very straight-forward project—it's really about ascending the stair from the ground level and arriving in the center of the house. Then there's a rooftop jacuzzi that pulls you up from the main floor and that again allows for these views in all directions.

The panoramic view takes over the experience of each space. We wanted the architecture to always maintain a relationship with—and a tension with—the view. We worked with a collage-type drawing that helped us think about the curvature of the exterior of the volume in relationship to the curvature of the walls. We liked how it begins to form a frame that relates the foliage of the trees to the profile of the distant mountains.

STUDENT: Is the house raised to emphasize the quality of the views or to establish privacy?

LEE: It's a bit of both, but I think the main priority is the view. The site is so vast that I don't think privacy would be a huge issue.

STUDENT: Would you say the rooftop jacuzzi is another way of introducing or creating a courtyard? This seems to be a prominent theme in your houses.

LEE: In some ways, yes. But this courtyard is also something that's nested within the project in a way. We like the contrast of being part of the vastness of the views while also being embraced by the house. It helps to contribute to the notion of compaction. The house is a literal result of stacking, but compaction is a driving force here.

STUDENT: Regarding the collage for this project, was there any intention about a conversation with or reference to Le Corbusier's Villa Savoye? Are you consciously expanding the idea of the ribbon window, the free plan, the relationship with the ground, or the rooftop garden? It's seems like these issues are all on the table and pretty explicit here.

LEE: All of them are on the table, yes, but not necessarily as an outward point or counterpoint to any sort of precedent. Le Corbusier and the five points are pretty much embedded in most of us. So sometimes it's just instinctive to relate to or make use of these strategies.

BIGHAM: There's an interesting question about legacies that we have to deal with and account for or try to overcome. I think students today certainly deal with Le Corbusier, but what are the other figures that you think students are trying to overcome? Who are the figures beyond the historical ones that you feel like you need to overcome?

LEE: I think parametricism is something that this generation is trying to overcome, but there are always these kinds of epidemics. The history of painting, especially in the U.S., is a series of epidemics and reactions. It's an evolutionary process. Sometimes what starts these processes or epidemics is an overestimation of something because it seems so new or different before the problems with it become apparent. I think with parametricism, people were excited by the new techniques and processes but then some of the issues began to emerge and the critics began to circle. What about you as students? Are there figures that you feel like you have to overcome?

STUDENT: OMA is among the candidates. But there's also Thom Mayne and the sort of contemporary California school of architecture—there's a lot of reaction to the gymnastics of that as well. I don't feel like we're compelled to move toward or away from any particular agendas or approaches though. I think the model here is to expose us to the spectrum of possible approaches and let us evaluate on a project-by-project basis while we develop our own interests and identities.

LEE: That's good. I think that's healthy. On the one hand, you need to be aware of the historical figures. On the other hand, you don't

want to be suppressed by them. I think what has happened in the 20th century is that the iconic, civic, and institutional buildings have gotten better while the 95% that's built by developers is getting worse. I think the question is whether a Zaha Hadid-designed opera house trickles down and forms a bigger and better everyday environment? I don't think it will and I think there are issues with this trickle-down mentality. I truly feel it's more important for architecture to be bottom-up and really establish the 95% while knowing that this 95% will not be a Zaha building. Architecture should not simply be about that remaining 5%, right? It's going to be a long road to work on this. At the same time, we cannot be cynical or overreact to the more iconic projects because sometimes you need those buildings. I just don't think that we should expect every project to deal with such demands.

JOHNSTON: Right. I think projects should be reactions to circumstances and problems, some of which are significant and not necessarily solved with such approaches. When I think about our Hill House, which was finished in 2004, it's in this canonical part of the Santa Monica Canyon. It was one of the few unbuilt parcels in this part of L.A. and was originally part of a much bigger property. In a sense, it was the bad leftover parcel. It's really steep. It's a 50% slope, so we knew that we needed to maximize the envelope.

This was originally a developer project. There were many constraints regarding how much volume we could generate. We started by working out how to maximize the envelope through a careful reading of the topography. As that idea evolved, we refined it to accommodate an opening for the car, which was really the most complex planning problem because of the relationship between the street and the slope.

We began to think about the house from the perspective of the view. It's an ideal panoramic view of Santa Monica Canyon. There's a real sense of the horizon through the middle floor of the house, which is the entry level. So the windows capture that sweeping panorama and then—because the house is a small parcel and close to its neighbors—there's another language of apertures as recessed windows that allow for more privacy. We use the thickened wall and the poche as a program for storage. This combination of sweeping panorama and a wall that almost dematerializes in relation to the deep cut window apertures is a precursor for some of our later projects.

Part of the economy of this project involved looking carefully at minimizing the expense of structure and how the building meets the ground. It's built on caissons with the house reaching 40 or 45

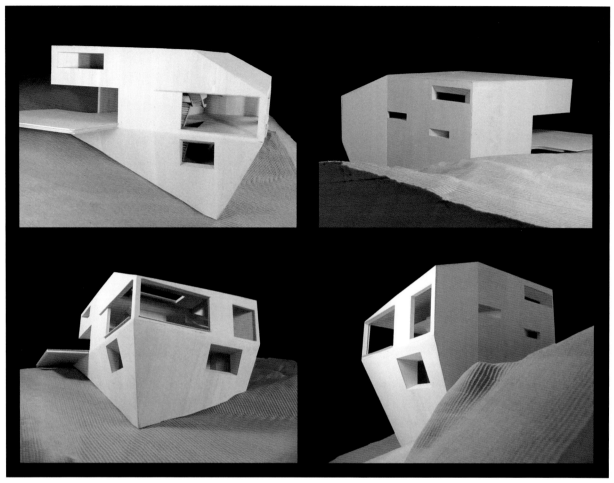

Hill House model

feet above ground. All of the caissons below reach a depth of 45 feet. So it's really 90 feet of structure from the base to the top of the roof and structure is expensive. Our strategy was to minimize the number of caissons down to nine; when our client originally bought the property, there was a project planned that had 23 caissons. So our project was very unconventional with lots of corners and a real focus on economy.

Related to structure, a couple of other things shaped this project. The envelope of the lower floor is lofted out from the small footprint with an incline that is precisely perpendicular to the slope. There's a cast-in-place wall. We were working in part to achieve literal compression, where we have a 90-degree-angle and a concrete floor that's tied back with tension rods to the caissons in the back of the house.

The facade to the street is a blank wall, which emphasizes the different ways that apertures can work between the recessed windows and the panoramic view. These types of contrast drive a lot of the thinking about this house.

LEE: The apertures were really important for us. We're certainly looking at Siza, and when you study Siza's work, you realize that all of the early projects were done for the communist party. It's low income housing and there's not much he can do; there are a lot of blank walls. When he does make an opening, he makes it super special and the whole plan and wall look magical. Later on, after the dictatorship is over, there's more money and he's building bourgeois houses, but I think it's good to understand the context of practices rather than seeing them as pure systems of artistic revolution or expression.

Early on, all of our houses were low budget projects, so we really look at walls and apertures. At that time in L.A., a lot of people were looking at using patterns where the window becomes part of a pattern, whether it's a razzle-dazzle pattern or something that would have windows that wrap around the corners. We weren't against that, but everyone was doing it so well that we wondered what the alternatives were. Rather than thinking of windows as part of a pattern, we began to consider them as part of a surface. We wanted to push the windows as deep as possible into the building. By doing so we use the poche to build cabinetry, but also to set the window back from the outer surface. This creates shade while preventing us from necessarily being hijacked by the window frame and the issues it can raise.

This attention to windows and patterns extends back to the beginnings of our practice. I remember looking through a book about international architecture and being able to tell which buildings were American and which were European just by looking at how thick the window frames were. European window frames are *this* thick and American window frames are *this* much thicker. So while we could make a thin window frame, it would be an uphill battle and we didn't have the budget for it. By pushing it in, the profile of the window comes back to the realm of architecture instead of being about product specifications.

Later on when the Hill House received an award, there were questions and criticism about the column in the corner on the main floor. Why it was there in the first place? Was it there to make that corner more heroic or something? In actuality, the column conceals a drainage pipe that moves water from the roof through the diagonal to the ground and then to the edge of the site where a sump pump moves the water to the street. Before the house was built there was a lot of water erosion from the current lot to the lower lot; building the house actually helps to preserve the lot below it. So that's the technical reason, but there's an aesthetic reason as well—it's important for that column to be there because it reminds you that it is the edge of the house. It is an indication that we built to the maximum edge of the envelope. We could not have an extended deck or an extended roof. The indoor-outdoor relationship here is very different from the mid-century case study houses where the floor just extends out or the roof just lifts up.

JOHNSTON: The idea for cladding for the house, given the three-dimensional way that we conceived of its form, was that we wanted a material that wouldn't delineate roof or wall in any kind of indexical way. The whole thing is a flexible and continuous membrane that coats all surfaces equally. It also allows us to avoid

Hill House

control joints and things that would have given it a dimension that would work against the manner in which we conceived of the three-dimensional figure.

LEE: The artist Jack Pierson consulted on the color. He noticed a lot of eucalyptus trees and suggested that we use the lavender color that sometimes shows up in the bark of the trees. It's a color that works well with the color of the leaves of the tree. So there's a very faint lavender tone that's worked into the cementitious material of the house. When the light is directly on it, it looks almost white, like a Greek building, but then around sunset the lavender will show up. We also used a lavender color on the door. For us, this color becomes something that makes the building seem alienated at certain moments, but then suddenly meshes back into the neighborhood as something familiar and contextual.

STUDENT: I have a question about this house and some of your other projects. I'm curious about the role that post-construction representation plays in them. It seems really important, from photographic documentation, to the illustration style, to the collaborative nature of the work with the artists you choose to work with.

JOHNSTON: Artists have been integral to our thinking about the buildings, but I think it's more important than that. Architects collaborate with a lot of people to build buildings. That's not anything new, but for us I think it's important that they work from a very different set of artistic questions. And whether it's literally within the building or part of the post-production work, I think it has helped us see the work through a different frame and has extended the conversation and understanding into other work and other disciplines.

We are trying to create a practice that understands the work in a more collective way. In some way, it's a relinquishing of control. Typically, when architects photograph their buildings, they're right behind the photographer and they're dictating a lot of what is captured. We've learned to prefer a form of collaboration where we remain open to other kinds of ideas that people can bring. We're looking for ideas outside of our own set of knowledge and familiarity. It's not a very conventional way for architects to work, but we've found a lot of value in it.

LEE: In the mid 90s, historians and theorists began to study the imagery of architectural representation, whereas historians before only studied the buildings themselves. So whether Le Corbusier leaves a hat or a pipe in an image for the sake of the documentation or if the photos make it look like someone was just there or that a group just left, it conveys a narrative when it comes to documentation. It starts to convey the notion that not everything was lined up and scripted. Of course, the imagery then takes on its own life and becomes another kind of work. We thought it was interesting to think about the building as having a life, not just as a physical building, but in such a way that there were other angles or aspects to the existence of it. Others contribute to that; it's not just the architect. When we say, hey, take this building and let us know what you think, one of the results is that the new collaboration—and the ideas that come from the collaboration—becomes one of the many characters in a script. It's interesting for us to see how artists will contribute to the script because some will treat it as a background and some will consider it a more active participant. Giving up that control can be difficult for a lot of architects.

STUDENT: How would you define *collaboration*? Is it between you and the collaborator? Between the collaborator and the building?

LEE: A great question. Some are more traditional collaborations. But in some cases, we finish something and pass it off. In the case of working with color, it usually happens during the design or construction process. In the case of post-production collaboration, we might explain the history and conception of the building and leave it to others. But there is such a thing as having or providing too much information, and you really want their input as opposed to their input-as-dictated-by-you.

STUDENT: I'm really excited to hear how you talk about the practicalities that go into the construction of a project because as architecture students, for the most part, we focus on the representation and design strategies. Design at that distance is not necessarily how things are going to stand up. The gutter on the

Hill House for example. To me, that's as much an elegant piece of work as the whole house in general. Is it difficult to work with consultants and structural engineers? When you said you wanted to go from 23 caissons to 9, did someone tell you you're crazy? I'm just interested in how you push for these ideas that are less conventional or pragmatic?

LEE: I think it's important to understand what you have at hand and what you're working with. Before we started the office, I spent a long time working in Switzerland where the construction cost per square foot is maybe four or five times that of the United States. With projects in Switzerland, they would zoom in and account for the fact that the screws are tightened and that they're all at the same angle, like a Cartier watch. There's no chance of achieving that level of precision here. So from the outset you have to think about the indigenous manner of construction that you're working with. I don't think you should think of it as a poor version of a Portuguese or Swiss building in California, though. It's going to be an American building. That's important. You need to understand the construction tolerance, which is part of why we think Frank Gehry is so good. It's not necessarily the forms he works with, though he is very good with the forms. It's that he just understands construction in a masterful way. It's hard to do an American building—especially a public building—because the sprinklers will be dealt with by one set of consultants, and then there's the exit sign consultant, lighting consultant, and HVAC consultant. How do you coordinate it to form something unified? It's a cacophony. Gehry knows that he can only fight certain battles, so he focuses architecture somewhere else and lets the exit signs be wherever. It's not slick in the same way that Thom Mayne is. Gehry leaves some tolerance, you know? His work has some humanity; it has flaws. For me, that's the brilliance with Gehry's work.

STUDENT: Do you do your own material tests and mockups or do you let consultants take that on?

JOHNSTON: We do a lot of mockups ourselves, but there's a lot of collaboration and testing between everyone involved in a project. This is something that we are pretty insistent on, literally, in terms of scheduling projects. We are always sure to leave enough time to do the mockups. We try to be very mindful of material and building technology and we strive to be ambitious about advancing certain kinds of detailing when we focus on certain aspects of a project.

LEE: While we try to plan ahead of time, sometimes we make on-site decisions. Not all diagrams of buildings are bulletproof once you actually start building. As the building becomes fatter or thinner, well-engineered things begin to change. Trying to control or anticipate these moments is important to us, but the reality is that you can't anticipate everything that happens. And the truth is that a project is rarely about isolated details or material studies. There is an understanding of context, intention, and history that is usually in the air as well.

STUDENT: Can you discuss the type of collage that you use to represent a lot of your projects?

JOHNSTON: You've seen the first collage of the Hill House. And you probably know the famous image of Craig Ellwood's house by Julius Schulman. And if you have seen that image by Schulman, you're aware of what we edited out of the image. We edited out the foreground, which is the cantilevered pool deck and the horizontal roof plane that extended out over the building. What we ended up with is this icon of a modernist midcentury interior hovering over this distant view.

When we were challenged and critiqued about the column in the corner, it really became an issue that was about this suspended room and the distant view. We used the history of that iconic image to rethink that condition in a contemporary house with different kinds of structural conditions. That kind of dialogue became an interesting part of the collages that we have made since. So we made this image and it got published and some friends who were lawyers said that maybe we should talk to Julius. [laughter] They thought he might not be happy about his image being remade. But we met with him and he was really lovely and said, "Of course I'll let you use the image, but you have to let me photograph the house when it's done." That was really the formal beginning of our collaborations with artists.

LEE: We love how the design of the house developed from a photograph and then became a photograph itself.

There's another project that brings up other issues: the Vault House in Oxnard, north of Los Angeles near Santa Barbara. It's not unlike many of the bay communities where all of the plots were zoned long and narrow to maximize properties on the beachfront. They're packed in like sardines. Most of these houses situate the living room facing the beach and the master bedroom on top facing the beach, which is great for those rooms, but then the rest of the house is dark and distant—and no one wants to be in those places. Furthermore, oftentimes you have to walk in between houses through an alley in order to find the front door, because

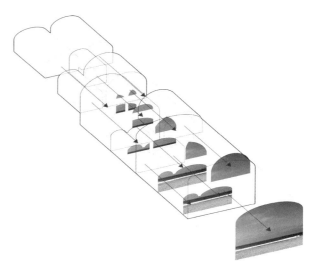

Vault House view diagram

the parking and garage will be out on the street front. So we knew we wanted to build a courtyard in the center of the house to offer a type of spatial decompression after walking through that narrow space between houses. We wanted a generous, open-to-above courtyard before you enter the house as the primary point of entry. The second thing we wanted to do was to bring as much view and air as deep into the house as possible.

The conceptual diagram of the house organizes space in a very pragmatic way. We gave every room a shape. In this case, the shape is a barrel vault and the barrel vaults are always open on each end. Basically, it's a series of shotgun house spaces mashed up together with the goal being that even when you are deep into the house you have a glimpse of the beach. Each of the diagrammatic vaults is symmetrical, but as a collection of vaults there's no shared axis between them.

We built a lot of physical models to study the character of both the house and the rooms. Each room being its own container is very important. The vaults never intersect one another; they're always just tangential. The moments where they meet are something that we became very interested in, but the directionality was the primary driver. I think that for us—planning-wise—this house is an important breakthrough because of the porosity and views that developed. A cylinder is a very directional volume, but you can't occupy floors in a cylinder, so the vaulted room is what we decided to work with. I think the street end fits in contextually, but the beach end is much more porous. This kind of contrast is something that will show up in other work later on.

Vault House, grid of rooms

We use upside-down vaults to make the clerestory windows. This is something that we came up with during development because we knew that the main source of views and air will be from the front. The side windows are always used for secondary or supplementary lighting. We initially worked with the idea of a right-side-up vault as a way to puncture the volume of the house. In doing so, like anywhere that you have a vault cut into another vault, we get a groin vault. Since we wanted to maximize the natural light coming in, we turned that condition upside down. So now the widest side cuts through the top of the vault, yielding a much wider cut—literally a greater dimension and more surface area— that allows more natural light in. Semantically, if someone says the house is like a piece of cheese or a sponge, I understand. But we never start off with a heuristic model of what the building should be. We started this project with very archetypal systems. In this case, the vault versus the arch. While it's true that the project took on a certain type of language or abstraction, it became the result of a process as opposed to existing as an *a priori* idea.

BIGHAM: How do you feel when people or critics put you or the work into various categories? Part of putting your work out into the world is knowing that it will be received in whatever way it's received. Do you read what others write about your work? Do you use that information in your practice?

LEE: I wish I could read them all. We're happy to participate because it puts us into taxonomies and frameworks that we may not have thought of before. Internally, I would say there's a desire for us not to be easily categorized because that puts walls around the practice. So maybe it's less about concern with what others say or think of us and more about the fact that it potentially creates a limited or limiting identity. We were educated at a time when our teachers and colleagues insisted that one must have a disciplinary project, that one has to define the project, and that this definition has to occur at the outset. I don't think you need to do that. I think it's important to try numerous strategies and approaches. Gehry has said he's tried on many jackets. He tried

Vault House south elevation

on Aalto and he tried on Le Corbusier and, after many tries, he learned what fit and what didn't.

When I look at history, I'm interested in these moments where people are in a group, yet outside of the group at the same time. If I look at the 1980 Venice Biennale and La Strada Novissima and all the postmodernists who are there: it's Ungers, Jencks, Isozaki, Venturi, etcetera. But then there's also Gehry and OMA, who are clearly outside of the group but are necessarily part of it. When the Postmodern starts to die, Gehry and OMA are still around. Even among their then-contemporaries, there was an interesting edge about their work, though it wasn't easily categorizable. Of course, you can understand how it was easy for the postmodernists to put them into their camp and say, "Gehry and OMA do some of the same things as us." I think eventually people will put boxes around you. That's okay, but I also think that you don't want to stay in those boxes for too long.

STUDENT: There's a very deliberate use of sequence and framing of views—or the lack of access to a view—in your work, especially in the houses. Can you talk about that?

LEE: Choreography of experience is important. With the Hill House, on the street side it looks like a one-and-a-half story building, but actually it's a three-and-a-half story building. We have a blank facade and tell people that we don't put windows there because it's a busy street, which is true. But we also want a blank facade as a prelude to the view within. We want the building to block the view and allow the user to discover the view behind it. This kind of veiling and unveiling is important for us.

The master of that is Mies Van Der Rohe, especially early Mies. The Tugendhat House is—for me—a much more important building than the Barcelona Pavilion. Don't get me wrong, the Barcelona Pavilion is brilliant in a number of ways, but it's a pavilion. In many ways, it's nonfunctional: you walk up a plinth and you see the universal space. But the Tugendhat House is a house: people actually live there. When you walk up and see the Tugendhat House, it's a one-story house. You have no sense that it's this kind of free plan manifestation downstairs, except for a slight protrusion of the eave. As you begin to move through the house, there are a series of moments that suggest something else is going on: the one cruciform column clad in rubber instead of chrome, the marble floor, the separation of volumes and spaces, the cellular packing of elements on the top floor. Then you go down a spiral stair. You enter straight-on and then you turn, and turn again, and then the universal space appears in front of you. It's so incredibly well done. We can talk about the Tugendhat House and about the universal space and how the glass windows slide here or there, the chrome, and all of the other details, but the choreography is what's massively important for me.

It's not only the argument of the space itself, but also how you get to that space. Good art transposes you from daily life and good architecture can transpose you from ordinary sequences of movement. What makes up or defines that threshold? Where's the interface between daily life and architecture? This question is key for us.

STUDENT: Typological elements and references show up in your work often, whether as walls, vaults, gables, and so on. Do you try to make the connection to these references visible?

Knoll, along Robertson Blvd.

LEE: For us, typologies and archetypes are basically the result of many years of history and evolution, which have become a built-in disciplinary intelligence. And we want to take advantage of that. I think it's a problem when it becomes a reference in the way I think you mean. It could become a reference when, for contextual reasons, all the houses have pitched roofs and yours is also a pitched roof. But the biggest problem with postmodernism is that it refers to something in an attempt to make a building more than what it is. The classic example would be that someone has designed a building and put a Palladian window in it. This doesn't make it a Palladian building. I think that illustrates where the gap between what something is and what something aspires to become cannot be too large. It's not that it's important for us to reference a typology overtly in the way that you suggest, but rather that these reference points give us the ground to begin working with.

A project related to this might be the Knoll Showroom in L.A. In an early scheme, every window had a different puncture and we were studying how the punctures become volumes. That idea never materialized because the landlord said there couldn't be any funny windows. That's because if the tenant moves out, they want minimum intervention to have to lease it. Having a certain neutrality was important for them. We end up having a series of volumes inside that are arches and vaults within or behind the windows. These vaults bring a different scale—something between room-scale and object-scale—to the framing of the furniture.

We got the idea from a director of Knoll in the 50s who took these modernist pieces by Bertoia and Saarinen to Morocco and shot them in a Moroccan house. There was this contrast between the old and the new that was kind of revolutionary at the time. We were looking at the shapes of the rooms and these Moroccan windows in contrast with the modernist furniture. We try to be aware of the references and use them as source material, but they're not something we're deferential to.

STUDENT: How does your design process change between residential and commercial work?

JOHNSTON: We recognize that commercial work usually needs to be much more adaptable. There's a different degree of specificity and program regarding how the space will be inhabited over time. We think of it more like a stage or platform than a collection of rooms, which is how our residential projects have evolved so far. It's more about the framing of an envelope of space and allowing something to be adaptable and to change every month or so if necessary. In the case of Knoll, the vault pieces create rooms within the larger room. They can be vignettes of smaller-scaled space or they can act like literal frames for objects.

BIGHAM: How do you define a house? I'm thinking more along conceptual lines because when there is a home owner-client, it's much clearer. Is it by scale? I've heard you talk about the Menil Drawing Institute as having a living room and using house terminology to discuss what is clearly a museum. Are there other aspects that determine that something is a house or house-like?

JOHNSTON: This is something that we are working on with larger-scale institutional projects. A room in a museum has to make an individual feel good if they're reading a book, but the space also has to be generous enough to accommodate a large group for a conversation and still perform well. I'm not sure if this exactly answers your question, but I think that intimacy and generosity are things that we're really striving to stay connected with when we work on bigger projects. We feel that intimacy and comfort are a prelude to engagement. Generous spaces provide that.

LEE: Being able to be alone while being part of a collective is important. James Turrell's work has always done this for me. I've always felt that his spaces allow me to feel both alone and isolated with the work yet very aware of my participation in that space with others who may be there. These are magical moments of isolation and collective occupancy. We try to give the houses that quality and we try to do the same with larger projects.

STUDENT: I have a question about typology. I want to clarify your point on it because you said it becomes a problem when it's merely a reference. With Knoll, I'm having trouble distinguishing how that isn't the case. How is that not simply appropriating that arch-vault form as a reference with all this history behind it?

LEE: I'm not saying our work doesn't have references. Some might say that the arches and vaults at Knoll are too much of a children's toy or too playful—but I have no qualms about what that space needs to be. For us, it's about creating an element that exists at an intermediate scale and that mediates between the piece of furniture and the larger space. That's it.

For certain architects, some projects start off simplistic and become complicated. I think that we start with something simplistic, make it complicated very quickly, and then try to make it simplistic again. Gehry also does this: he starts with a box and then he starts to put something on top and it starts to crumble. It becomes complicated and then it gets smoothed out again.

STUDENT: In terms of economy of form, it really seems like you apply limits on what to work with: arches, primitive shapes, boxes, vaults, cylinders. Do you recognize this as an issue? It's the closest thing to a signature that I can think of.

LEE: Like everyone else, we want to do relevant things that make sense for the climate that we exist in, and for us that means not being ironic. It's about not imposing anything on you. We like our buildings to be like people, with depth and with something mysterious about them: the more you inquire and probe, the more that gets revealed. It's not about being loud or too in your face, because a lot of the time being loud doesn't necessarily mean you have much to say. We think that having a more limited means makes it much more accessible, as opposed to showing virtuosity so overtly. There are those who say, "Look what I can do with all this and still juggle at the same time." That might be interesting for a short period, but I'm not convinced of its longevity.

JOHNSTON: I think one of the other things about the economy of these forms is that they result in spaces that allow for a generous occupation of the room or building. They can support different lifestyles or modes of living. Maybe this answers Ashley's question about the definition of a house, but I think there needs to be a certain generosity of space that isn't overly rigid in how you can use it or furnish it or how many people can be in it. It should feel warm and domestic regardless.

LEE: I agree. Not all architecture needs to be so overt or present. Sometimes when that is the case, nothing is possible. Andy

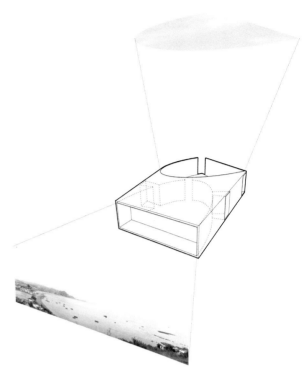

META Chile House view diagram

Warhol said that if everything is art, nothing else is possible and if there's no art, everything is possible. We try not to think about a particular style because that's what the generation before us was about. We try to start every project fresh. Of course, after you've been in practice for 20 years, there are certain architectural problems that you think about a lot, and habits will form—whether it be about apertures or economies of form—and that starts to build up into its own collection of knowledge. We're not fighting this reality, but we try to make appropriate choices with each project. The kinds of questions that arise in school about being a contextualist or non-contextualist? If you build in Venice or Rome, the context and history are incredibly important, but if you build in suburbia in Columbus your architecture is the context. Learning when to assert certain strategies and when to sit back is something that takes time to learn. But I think it's important to learn it.

JOHNSTON: A good example is the META Chile House, which came about in 2010 after a pretty severe earthquake in Chile. In disaster relief situations, housing is always the first program that you need to satisfy. Our building was intended to be dwelled in— temporarily, if desired—but it could have been a school or some kind of small cultural building beyond that. There were a number of

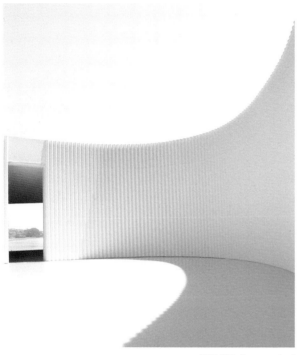

META Chile House courtyard META Chile House model

offices invited to develop different sites, and our particular site was in a pine forest that was up on a bluff looking out over a bay. The brief called for a building that was a couple thousand square feet.

For us, the beauty of the site was really important—it's really quite dramatic. We knew we wanted to amplify the programmed area, so we began to think about doubling it and creating an exterior room that was more of a courtyard. In thinking of the courtyard as a room oriented toward the sky and the pavilion as a room with a view toward the bay, it began to emphasize a dual quality of being both a highly pragmatic building and one that has a special feature that emphasized or allowed for reflection on that moment in the history of the country.

The first space you enter is open to the sky—it's a clearing in the trees—and is one of two ellipses that are connected at a tangent; they're hinged at this one point. The poche space between the ellipses holds other programmatic elements. The other ellipse holds the view out toward the bay. The facade simply wraps those forms. It's really very mute, almost like a bunker.

We did have to clear a few trees to make space for the building and we thought about their trunks as a way to commemorate a

deeper connection to the site, so we used them to develop a mold form. The scallops in the corrugated material on the surface of the courtyard wall are meant to mark the traces of those trees from the landscape.

In contrast to this heavy texture in the courtyard, with the interior space we were interested in bringing the view deeper into the interior of the building, beyond the framed view itself. We began thinking about how we could simply polish the walls to get this hazy horizon or reflection that would sweep around the interior.

LEE: The relationship between the space and the framing of the distant view is really important. The first courtyard is rough and has a vertical rhythm, and then you walk into this room with a magnificent view out. Of course, the first thing you see is the view, but we try to make people conscious of the fact that the room is a half ellipse or amphitheater, and that you're embraced by this horizon line encircling you. The siting on the bluff is almost at the edge, and the space is like a theater that is projected out. This is an important project for us even though it's very humble; it speaks volumes about how we can interact with a site. At 3,000 square feet, it's tiny. How do we capture the reality of this place? It's a very simple building but very focused on sequence and specific moments.

STUDENT: I'm curious about how your shift from a focus that might deal with structure or form moves to addressing different textures or materials. The early projects seem less interested in those concerns.

JOHNSTON: I wouldn't say it's a shift. When I think about the context in which we've built up our practice, there's a certain kind of L.A. school that's built on a type of material eclecticism—whether that's Mayne, Rotundi, Moss, or Gehry's earlier work. We saw that as a significant part of the legacy of the generations before us, and we wanted to try something else. In our earliest projects, materiality wasn't at the forefront of our focus. But also, those projects are very low budget and we were just more focused on structure and aperture at that point. There just wasn't enough money to go around and make in-depth material studies. Space and structure were simply where we started.

LEE: I also think it's important to not feel like you have to reinvent everything. It's true that some of these issues were less often addressed early on. But both then and now, we feel that not everything needs to be undertaken with the same intensity. Not everything needs to be interesting or foregrounded. The quotidian things make the interesting ones more interesting.

In 2013, we took part in the Shanghai West Bund Biennale. We were invited to do the Pavilion of Six Views for an exhibition and they wanted this building to be permanent, but they didn't tell us what it was going to be. [laughter] They said it could eventually become a restaurant, a cafe, an office building, or a showroom. We thought of the Chile House, where we had the two volumes, and asked, "What if we have more?" Because the prospects for each of the buildings are comparable: they are built to serve an immediate need but may become something else down the line. It became simple. We have six volumes instead of two. Three of them are internalized and form a triangle courtyard. The other three are extroverted, framing different views of the site. The three that face outward have a hinging relationship with the three that face inward. It's pretty straightforward. There are always two sources of light: the skylight and the window that faces the view. Entry always happens at the crevice where the inward-facing pavilion meets an outward-facing one. Sometimes the building seems expanded and sometimes it seems quite attenuated.

After the biennale was over, it was abandoned for a bit before it became the Shanghai Center of Photography. Of course, if we had known that this would be the eventual program, we would have incorporated more straight walls because the walls that are

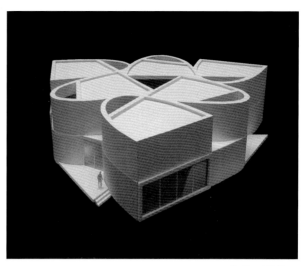

Pavilion of Six Views

there can't display large format photography. There's also the issue of light. Older prints are light sensitive and the skylights aren't necessarily ideal.

STUDENT: You continue the idea of scalloped surfaces from the Chile House onto this project. Did it have anything to do with this particular site?

LEE: Correct, we did. This project came in at the end of the Chile House, so the ideas were carried over—quite directly in some cases. But this is also a project where the site is not quite a site. It's a former industrial area that was just empty at the time. We knew that it would eventually be built up with high rises and commercial space and institutional space. But with it being empty, we have an opportunity to provide context instead of responding to context. We get to make the first move, like a chess match where our piece is the only one on the board. That's a fairly uncommon scenario, but one that lends some forms of freedom.

STUDENT: Each of you come to architecture with a rather unique background. Are there any obscure or secret references or precedents that you find yourself coming back to? It seems like Western architectural education tends to come back to the same references over and over again.

LEE: Off the top of my head, I don't think of it as West versus East or anything like that, it is more about being interested in things outside of architecture. We've always been interested in fine arts, contemporary art, and so on. We are always interested in industrial

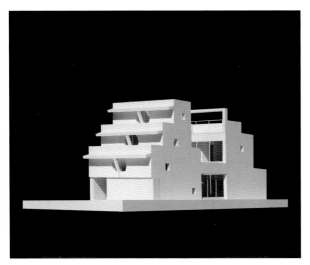

Canal House

The Pavilion of Six Views is a good expression of our interest in the module as a single unit that forms the foundation for an alphabet, and this of course has origins with the Chile House. On one hand, the individual units are fragmented parts that are grouped together. On the other hand, they create a universal geometry that unites everything together. There's a part-to-whole condition that we're always interested in. When we discuss the spanning projects, you'll see that there's a certain point where the whole is very hard to keep together. In some cases, we need something larger to help us organize. How many parts does it take to start to see a whole and how many instances does it take to understand the presence of a group? I think these are some of the questions that we try to address frequently in our work. This project is a good example and the issue pertains to both objects and spaces.

The Canal House is in Kyoto, Japan. It's a three-level concrete construction along a canal lined with cherry blossom trees. We were looking to Le Corbusier and Barragán for different ways to make outdoor rooms. We began thinking about a much more introverted space, but we were also considering traditional Japanese windows that are round and cropped. We have a canopy with a single support, and the canopy is made of concrete and spans the entire width of the house. The elements are very thick and contribute to a very compacted series of spaces.

In the center of the house is a courtyard, but you don't enter the courtyard from the front. You enter the house from the front and then walk past the courtyard and into the living room in the back. On the other side of the courtyard is a traditional tatami room.

STUDENT: How do you deal with the connection between the traditional tatami room and the rest of the house? How do you keep them separate?

JOHNSTON: It's like a capsule.

LEE: Right. Typically, this kind of room has to be located in a part of a house where some guests might arrive, but you're not necessarily going to invite them into the deeper main house. They will take off their shoes and you can have tea or sake, but it's almost more of a formal business transaction area.

JOHNSTON: In addition to the tatami room, there's a special tree in the courtyard that's also part of the visual landscape that unifies the dwelling space with the shared view from the tatami room. There are some basic standards for creating a traditional

design and fashion design. Other interests—whatever they are— give us a parallel way of understanding what we are and what we do. We're interested in art because we also have no vested stakes in that world. We have friends in it, but we are actually not part of the art world. So it's nice be able to exist like that, almost as an outsider looking in.

JOHNSTON: I think we're always very clear that we don't see ourselves as artists. We're always very much operating at the core of our own discipline. As Mark said, there's a sort of otherness about these other worlds and disciplines that is both physically, materially, and intellectually valuable to us. There's a real insularity about the world of architecture. It's a big world in some ways, but it's also often inwardly-oriented. It's been really healthy for us to be part of other communities that track into a larger cultural discourse.

LEE: I think it's important to know history and also to know something outside of your world. Marcel Duchamp was a good enough chess player to represent France in national competitions. Yves Klein was a judo master and wrote a book about judo. John Cage is known for being a brilliant experimental musician, but he was also an expert on mushrooms and fungi to the point where he wrote articles that contributed to their study and understanding. No one asked him how he became interested in mushrooms until he was interviewed late in his life. It turns out that he was just fooling around and decided to look in the dictionary for a word that came before *music* and it was *mushrooms*. He decided to become an expert on that. Whatever the reason is for finding an obsession, I think it's a good idea to get outside of your discipline.

space. The procession that Mark described is designed so that people don't get too far into the private dwelling of the house.

LEE: The interior courtyard is much more modern with as much glass as possible. Everything is quite transparent. Only the exterior has the traditional windows. From the master bedroom you can look through the courtyard into the master study with the traditional window. There are layers of views and lighting that pass through the whole set of spaces.

STUDENT: The cantilevers are right in front of the window?

LEE: Yes. With the traditional Japanese window, the canopy is an element that could actually hinge and fold down. When propped up, they put a wooden stick in place to hold it up. We just made it permanent. We liked the round shape of the window frame and right in front of it, we placed the post. The canopy itself slopes down, directing the view to the canal.

JOHNSTON: Since that view focuses on the canal, it was important to have a rooftop space with a view toward the mountains, which are very symbolic. When you're inside the living spaces, it's an inward-oriented view of the courtyard and the rest of the house.

The UIC Center for the Arts at the University of Illinois in Chicago is a competition between us, Morphosis, and OMA. The campus was designed by Walter Netsch of SOM and was known for a kind of organic construction that works as a field. Later on, this idea was abandoned as more modernist buildings came in. But generally speaking, these buildings are quite hated by both the administration and the students. The ideas of stacking and ziggurat-like forms were in our heads at the time, and we wanted this project to have a similar massing to the buildings that were done before by Netsch, but that were much more transparent and translucent and had a lightness to them.

We used the ziggurat as a type and then reversed it and used an upside-down ziggurat as well. We grouped these self-similar forms together for the two theaters and connected them by way of a public foyer. The volumes have a translucency that allows you to see the fuchsia-red theaters that are hidden behind a screen. Fuschia is the color of UIC. There's also an industrial language: there's a canopy that demarcates the entry, almost akin to the loading zone of a warehouse. The skin is all perforated metal panels.

STUDENT: It's interesting to see the progression of your work and how it has gone from a more structural approach and organizational agenda to one that is more focused on ideas of materiality and transparency. How did that come about?

LEE: We realized that the scale of institutional and cultural projects is often too severe to be completely solid. It's a scale that needs a certain humanity, whether through the breaking down of volumes, having different details at the architectural scale, or having different degrees of translucency. I think the scalloping on the perforated metal panels softens the edges of the geometry.

JOHNSTON: Maybe this is a good moment to talk a little bit about detailing. Rem Koolhaas has written about the idea of not having details and an effort to not put a lot of focus on how materials come together. It leaves a certain kind of abstraction and material expression that you can focus on. For example, the poche between the perforation on the surface and the boxes behind was productive in that there was circulation and other program elements. We made pretty good use of the doubling between the glass box and the metal and theater boxes. It also allowed us to accommodate a very banal curtain wall and then have a repetitive detail that we could master and control. There was an important degree of economy in that it produces effects without a lot of complexity.

STUDENT: It seems consistent with a lot of contemporary discourse, which tends to think of poche as no longer restricted by a need to be structurally driven. It enables a wall to move from building performance to architectural performance.

JOHNSTON: Except in this case I would argue that the poche performed in both ways. We use it to get daylight in as well as to evacuate heat. It also allowed us to isolate the concert halls that had very precise acoustic needs relative to the rest of the building. So the doubling or multiplying of the skin met criteria for both the building performance and the visual or architectural performance you are talking about.

LEE: One of the things I love about this project is that if you squint, you can read the mass of the whole but is has very fuzzy edges. It has a strength of center that exists in contrast to the fuzzy edge in space, and there's something interesting about that. You can feel the shape, but the shape is not sharp.

STUDENT: You have between 70 and 90 built projects. Do you think about the commercial work as a way of developing ideas? Looking at those smaller projects, it seems like you tested out ideas that you came back to. Are you still able to do that?

JOHNSTON: Yeah, absolutely. Those projects have a very different cadence than the competitions and cultural projects, which have a really long timeframe. For the mental health of the office and the ability to experiment and do things quickly, those projects continue to be important. It's a bit harder to do them now because we have big teams working longer term on larger projects.

STUDENT: It seems like with a lot of offices, once big projects start coming along there are fewer and fewer boutique projects. How do you keep the small projects while still being able to take on the larger ones?

LEE: I think it's a management question more than a desire question. This is part of architectural practice that doesn't get a whole lot of discussion. When the 2008 financial crisis came, how did offices like ours manage? We have these projects, but it's 20 small projects that bring the same income, whereas previously four or five projects would provide the same. With 20 projects, the amount of administration goes up exponentially. For us, that's a losing deal. But you have to do it because that's where the economy is. The economy moves for better or for worse, and sometimes projects that you expect to be there get shelved—either permanently or for years. How do we feed the people that we hire? It's an economical question about the ability to make use of what you have available to you.

JOHNSTON: But you're right. You need a lot of intelligence in your office and those small projects are a way to train young architects to know how to do things when the stakes are lower. Some people in our office have been with us for 15 years and are now running very large projects, but they grew up in a sea of all these small projects, which is helpful in developing our team in every aspect.

We really try to build a community with clients and the arts community and we frequently do multiple projects for an individual client. We try to build a shared understanding. We don't just do one and move on—we try to build trust and test ideas. Cultivating great clients takes work and effort. Sometimes that starts with small projects. We travel a lot with our clients. We look at shows together. We eat together. Building relationships is important to building the trust you need in order to experiment. It's not always the typical trajectory of schematic design to construction documents. We really do try to build a culture around the projects we work on.

BIGHAM: I have a question that has more to do with logistics and day-to-day operations. What's typical day like for you? In any practice there's a travel component, but now the practice is bi-coastal. So there's a travel component, the education component where you're teaching, an academic leadership position, an office with one or two physical locations, projects that are all over the world, and an office full of employees that you're trying to develop. And then there's your personal lives. How do you structure your time and what have you found that works well for you and the practice?

LEE: The main office is in Los Angeles and there's a satellite office in Cambridge. Obviously, we're partners and we're both involved in all of the projects, but oftentimes as a project evolves, one of us will be the partner in charge and it just has a lot to do with who has the time and maybe who develops more rapport with the client.

When a project gets to construction documentation, Sharon is usually more involved. I'll be involved more peripherally. This is a common cadence of the office. When I took the leadership position at Harvard, we saw it as an opportunity for people that had been with us for a while to step up and take on different degrees of responsibility. At times, being in Cambridge has been a challenge for me—especially for the projects in L.A.—because regardless of the technological tools and how savvy I try to be with them, it's very different from being able to immediately deal with issues. That's one of reasons we work with physical models, because there's a material resistance and you can see it and touch it. No matter how many cameras we have looking at a thing, it's no surrogate for actually being there. However, the Cambridge office has been good for its proximity to Miami and Philadelphia and New York.

JOHNSTON: Our office isn't exactly formulaic. Each project has its own alchemy and DNA and people, and spending time in the library is one of the ways that people succeed in the office. As we grow and get bigger projects, we're having to become smarter about how we transfer knowledge in the office because not everyone has developed in that setup over the last 15 years.

LEE: We know who we are because of the people that we have and we really invest in our team. We're not an office that routinely runs 60 or 70 hours a week; we work very normal hours. So maybe that is a partial answer to Ashley's question about one way in which we try to manage our personal lives and allow others to manage theirs. When we have a deadline, we work on weekends, but we're not crazy. We want people to be with us for a long time and we recognize that a work-life balance is really important. We

know that in the first six to nine months, an individual is not going to be very productive for the office. We know it takes time. We don't care which programs you know, because you'll learn what you need to as you grow. We're a very slow office when it comes to growth, but it has worked well for us. Sometimes it has meant we don't take on projects. This isn't necessarily a philosophy that would work for everyone.

JOHNSTON: There's an intensity about each project that means we just can't do 30 big projects. There's a lot of research and development that goes into each project, especially when it's a type of project that doesn't have a precedent within the context of the practice. There's a lot of intellectual energy that goes into building a culture around a project and we invest a lot of time there, especially during the early phases.

STUDENT: How should we as graduates gain agency in the field when we leave school?

JOHNSTON: There are so many paths into the discipline right now. There are so many types of practitioners. Just remember that it takes a long time, even though the cycles for your generation are moving much faster. Architecture is one of the few old professions that's still slow; it takes a long time to develop ideas and build buildings and it's expensive. In some ways, everything is working against evolution and contemporary culture.

Sometimes it's not that glamorous, but what's exciting for us is when we realize we've had some people for 10 or 15 years and that they are so dedicated and so generous with others. There are moments when a certain mastery that they have just becomes available and then they're able to communicate that knowledge. And at times, it literally happens overnight. Just remember that it takes time, and remember to keep building knowledge in as many areas as you can.

LEE: And remember to identify what is good and to get the most out of a situation, even if you're not happy being at a certain office or whatever. Ask yourself, "What does this firm do well?" Maybe it's not design. Maybe it's management. Maybe it's developing relationships with contractors. Focus on those things, because there is always something you can get from any situation.

STUDENT: What are your thoughts on the role of drawings doing work that architecture cannot? Of the performance that drawings and representation can produce outside of the architecture or independent of the built project?

LEE: There are a lot of models that we currently teach and look at: Koolhaas, Venturi, Rossi. These are architects and theoreticians. And they're great at both. But I don't think that everyone should be a singer-songwriter or feel compelled to be so. As educators, we shouldn't force these things. We should expose students to ideas with the understanding that there are very good singers who should not write and very good writers who should not sing.

If we look back at moments of history—like postmodernism—when the economy was booming, there's no real urgency and it becomes a luxury to talk about language and style in architecture. In moments of luxury, we can explore these things en masse, but in moments of crisis, architecture needs to step up. One of the questions for you as students who are about to enter the world is, "What is the moment right now for you? What are we looking at?"

I'm very interested in architectural representation. I'm curious about it as a niche area of study too. There are schools and schools of thought that are obsessed with it to the point that the built environment or the building doesn't matter. For me, that's a problem. I'm okay with the idea that someone wants to focus on that and be an artist. That's okay. I think it's a problem for the world of architecture when that becomes the expectation or when that approach takes over working on the actual building or space. That's one of the reasons why, for collaborative projects outside of the building or for developing certain aspects of a building, we work with people in the art world. We want someone who has their feet firmly planted in that world, as opposed to saying that we can do both with equal degrees of expertise. Our disciplines are adjacent and there is a lot of crossover, but they are simply not synonymous.

STUDENT: What are your thoughts on the role of film in architecture as related to representation? The flythrough? I'm suspicious of it but it seems pretty pervasive.

LEE: Because it's too prescriptive?

STUDENT: It doesn't give you the experience of the space. You get the bird's eye view and then it will usually swoop down and around, but who experiences a building that way? So maybe these are just more for a client or developer?

JOHNSTON: Sounds like a choreography problem...

STUDENT: But how many visits to any building are so prescriptive? It's one of the difficulties I have: I want to script variation into any representation of this sort.

LEE: There's a question of duration. Not material duration, but rather the unfolding of the experience. I read an article about the model Kate Moss and the longevity she has had in her field. She's very elusive and it seems like there's something hidden about her. It's why so many photographers, editors, and artists are drawn to her. It's been hard to say exactly what she was or who she was and there has always been something a little edgy and dangerous about her that made her exciting and interesting. A lot of fashion and modeling is based on the ability to project fantasies, and Kate Moss has facilitated that for those who work with her.

I would say that not showing everything or putting everything on the table is really important. Over time, you discover that you can map different durations of time because different cadences emerge for different users. I think this is something that one could plan or project. All buildings should have that type of richness, but the issue with the flythrough is one that deserves a fair degree of critique.

STUDENT: But a still image becomes a rendering of its own, right? It can be just as scripted. I'm trying to figure out how to show episodes and thresholds that express different experiences. I like places where something can be revealed or hidden. I like the idea that a body can be forced along a path or allowed to meander. Representation can allow for those kinds of freedom. The tricky part is having to step back from trying to control things all the time and control the path or control the user. It's a difficult equilibrium to find.

JOHNSTON: What about the technique of the film still? How is that different than looking at a continuous movement through a building? How could you use the gaps and that kind of sequencing as opposed to the continuity? I tend to think of Herzog & de Meuron in terms of a collection of moments, and of OMA as a sequence through spaces. In either case, how one controls scale, focus, and depth of field can produce different results or degrees of control. There's also the notion of modifying duration so that it's not continuous, like splicing.

BIGHAM: The office has amassed enough work at this point that there must be internal conversations that drive the work. Things that you guys keep coming back to? I think that early on in a lot of creative careers it seems like artists are doing these things but also keeping an eye on the outside world and trends that are taking form. Are there certain questions in the office that are like this that you can talk about?

LEE: As in, is the set of issues closed or open?

BIGHAM: Sure. It seems like you're working out internal questions. The work is very distinctive. It's a coherent body of work even with the amount of variation that it has. Obviously, portions of questions come back again and again. It seems that, on the one hand, you pay attention to what's going on in the world, but on the other hand, the office has some topics or problems that it keeps working on. Do you recall when you developed the confidence in your own work to take on internal questions as opposed to looking outside to make sure you're hitting the mark?

LEE: I think the topics Sharon outlined at the beginning is our attempt to categorize the issues we see coming up again and again. Compaction, hinging and stacking, and spanning are all things that show up repeatedly. With more recent work, the problem of framing or of the frame represents a theme that is consistently present. I like the idea that we try on different jackets. But after a while you see what fits you and what doesn't: it's trial and error, and then it becomes a set of directions. This is something that's subconscious no matter how much we want to avoid a certain distinct signature or style. After a while, certain things that you look at often—whether it be apertures, typological profiles, or whatever—begin to emerge in the work.

JOHNSTON: The idea of spanning first emerged as an approach for some early competitions. Usually it has to do with big roof projects. It indicates a shift in the scale in our work. We were looking for methods to start organizing larger spaces or territories, so it tends to show up as a collection of smaller buildings clustered under a big roof. There's still an idea of the building as an object, but it widens the scope to become a dialogue between the idea of a big roof and the idea of the small pavilion.

LEE: It's the roof as an organizational system. The Hut House is in Hawaii, very close to the sea with strong trade winds that impose themselves. It's among the wettest and most humid places in the world and a lot of the traditional houses have a porch that surrounds the entire house. We organized the whole thing so that we have the same amount of exterior space as interior space. It's evenly split and it's organized as four smaller houses or volumes grouped under one roof with a courtyard in the middle. The area is stylistically controlled, and there are only a few types of roofs that one can use, so we use a traditional Hawaiian pitched roof and rotate it slightly. The volume of the roof in relationship to the four houses underneath is such that when the cuts happen, they're unique in terms of the height of the roof in relationship to the spac-

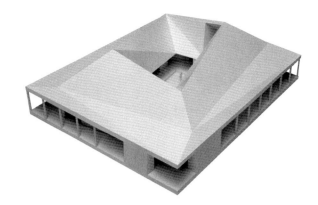

Hut House

Green Line Arts Center

es below. It's a very museum-like building, with separate locations and a focus on how light gets into the spaces below.

JOHNSTON: The Green Line Arts Center is a competition from 2015. It's just west of The University of Chicago, adjacent to Washington Park. The project was developed with Theaster Gates, an African American artist from the south side of Chicago who has been doing a lot of development work in the area. The goal was to develop a contemporary art center for dance, performance, and film, and to put it all within an existing building that was pretty much just a facade or shell at the time.

The project is a rebuilding or repairing of the local urban fabric as part of an arts neighborhood. Our approach was to insert a new roof based on a very common vernacular: it's a simple serrated, industrial roof shed that results in a modular building system that houses large halls for the performance spaces and open winter garden spaces. The idea behind a simple, repetitive structure was that it would not only create the enclosure for the building, but also start to spread out and create work yards that nest into the

Green Line Arts Center massing and roof

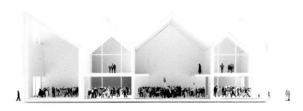

Simulation diagram, Green Line Arts Center multifunctional halls in use

backyard of the adjacent buildings. This approach gave us a tool to spread out and create a bigger landscape for the building.

We really wanted a solution that would address both the industrial identity of the area and the residential presence around the neighborhood—there are a lot of large warehouses around. That legacy was more important to us than installing an icon of a building, and it just made more sense given the local fabric. The profile of the roof becomes something that marks it as distinct relative to the surrounding buildings. The modules of the roof define the spaces underneath: studio spaces and black box theatres with two winter gardens as flux spaces for performances, meetings, and community programming. The walls that define these spaces can be opened up to create one continuous space.

LEE: I'll add that the winter gardens are not called for in the program. For us, these are spaces that you'll also find in the Menil Drawing Institute or the UCLA Margo Leavin Graduate Art Studios. These are unprogrammed spaces but we see them as third spaces that could be attached to the cinema, the black

box theater, or opened up to the adjacent street. They allow the program to fluctuate from one side to the other. We see this as an expansion of the building itself.

JOHNSTON: It's an approach that we try to take to both arts and non-arts spaces. With the historic facade, we really just opened it up so that it's a little more transparent. The clerestory windows that sit above that facade mark a new scale for the building behind it but it still sits quietly in this repetitive fabric of the other buildings that have the same historic facade treatment. In a very casual way, the building opens back up to the street, which was a really important part of the mission for this project. It needed to have a reciprocity between the front and the back. The proposal doesn't express the traditional hierarchy of the front entry; the back is just as welcoming and just as important to the sense of the identity of the building as the front.

We also imagined this modular system developing the entire block where these structures could spread out and claim more territory on the block or in the neighborhood, becoming a series of indoor and outdoor spaces that draw direct interaction from the streets and sidewalks and add to those conditions.

LEE: Similarly, we were commissioned to do a schematic study for the MOCA in Los Angeles that was designed by Arata Isozaki. It originally opened in 1986, but now you have the Disney Concert Hall by Frank Gehry, the Broad Museum by Diller, Scofidio, and Renfro, Moneo's cathedral, Coop Himmelblau's school, and the existing Dorothy Chandler pavilion from the 50s. So the whole neighborhood has been pretty much completed.

When this museum was initially finished, it was like a ship on a dry dock. There was nothing around, there was no context. The museum essentially represents Isozaki's tropes from that time: very prismatic forms, the barrel vault, the pyramids, Indian red sandstone, a gestural Corbusian-like curve, and a crushed glass wall. A number of things were added later on, like a glass canopy and a bunch of sculptures that began to permeate the park. But with everything else that had been built, the building no longer had much of a presence. It was like a little village that had been lost amongst the skyscrapers. We went back and looked at Isozaki's original drawings. They had very strong features: long shadows, really prismatic, bold volumes. This got us thinking about how we could bring back these qualities.

The first phase deals with how to renovate the building and the second phase deals with adding onto the building. The scattered

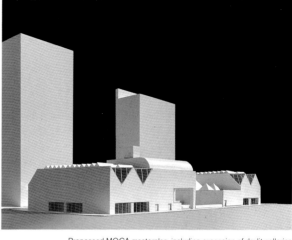

Propossed MOCA masterplan, including expansion of daylit galleries   Proposed MOCA masterplan, including expansion of daylit galleries

collection of volumes and program created a number of ineffi-ciencies. There were problems with wayfinding. Oftentimes, a line of people blocks the pathway of individuals going to the shop or trying to get to the plaza, or people go into the shop and ask them where to get tickets. For us, it was very straightforward—almost as simple as cleaning up what had been added on. We relocated the ticket office to the lower level. We added a wall, which helped to define the plaza and allowed us to dictate how people arrive. When you arrive at the plaza, you have arrived at MOCA. So again, the idea of the courtyard becomes a very important part of the project and a transition between the city and the spaces we are responsible for.

In order to add to the museum, we took the form of a small build-ing that Isozaki did in L.A. from around the same time as MOCA. The form looks like a pitched-roof house, but it's actually not. It has two cuts on the corners that allow for really beautiful sky-lights. We took that as a point of departure and multiplied it, using the idea of spanning as applied to a field. It was an interesting way for us to use an Isozaki trope and transform it in a different way to work with the volumes that he used from 1986. I think our goal was to do something where, if you visit the building for the first time and don't know the history, you don't quite know what is new and what is old.

JOHNSTON: Another project that deals with the legacy of site and pre-existing buildings and contexts is the Menil Drawing In-stitute. The Menil campus is about 30 acres. There are two Renzo Piano buildings, the Rothko chapel, a Byzantine chapel, the Dan Flavin installation building, and a large apartment building that

was a source of revenue for many years for the campus. So it's a series of satellite structures scattered about that define a loose neighborhood of art that emerges out of a very understated and suburban neighborhood.

All of these buildings have been defined by a particular way that natural light comes into the galleries from above. They're all very different kinds of art viewing experiences, but that's the legacy of the Menil. Connecting the institutional buildings are a series of variously-scaled gardens that are punctuated by works of art. It's a very informal residential neighborhood. People are hanging out, walking their dogs, having picnics. This is largely because of a col-lection of bungalow buildings that the institution has bought over the years, many of which are used for their various programs and are rented out. They're all painted the same gray color, which lends it a kind of neutralizing feeling that creates a sense of place, but there's not a lot of signage or anything that would define it as an institution. The final layer is the presence of these beautiful trees that have been cultivated over the years that give the area a kind of shady coolness. So the campus is made up of these buildings that are nested within a collection of gardens and vernacular houses and together that's what defines the Menil collection.

Our building is the Menil Drawing Institute. It's about 30,000 square feet, so it's relatively small by institutional standards. We always thought about our building as a hybrid between the Menil Collection building by Piano and the house that Phillip Johnson did for the Menils in the early 50s. The Piano building has beautiful galleries, but also a number of exterior spaces that are quite nice. The Menils had spent an extended period of time in Caracas,

Menil Drawing Institute courtyard

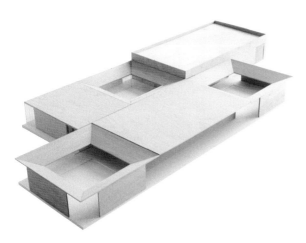
Menil Drawing Institute model view from southwest

Menil Drawing Institute west entry courtyard

Venezuela, and the tropical garden landscape was an inspiration they brought into the design of their house. The courtyard in the house really is the defining room, and all of the public spaces of the house surround it.

The idea of a building dedicated to drawings was a relatively unprecedented building type, especially in the U.S. We had to piece together a lot of research by visiting study centers and drawing galleries, mostly within larger museum buildings that were dedicated to more encyclopedic collections. Our conceptual approach was to use a thin roof that would spread into the landscape among many of the existing trees. This provided some shaded structure for the exterior spaces as well as the contents of the museum.

First, we mapped a number of the existing trees that were part of the legacy of that apartment complex. We started by creating rooms around these trees as outdoor gardens and thresholds between the site, the larger campus, and the interior of the building. The building then fits in between those gardens and forms the three primary programs of the Institute, which consists of an exhibition gallery, a study center for scholars, and a conservation lab that doubles as an archive for drawing storage. In the interior of the building, the rooms were calibrated to the scale of the works on paper. The average size for drawings in their collection is around 18 by 24 inches, so the majority of the work is quite small. We view the building as sitting in a relationship to the bungalows that form the primary necklace of the main campus—its stature comes quite close to those.

The Menil Collection has always had a tradition of social justice and of working with really diverse artists and practices from cultures around the world, so there was always a sense that programs and spaces could sort of unfold because of the proximity of things. You might not necessarily have a dance in a theater building; there has always been a loose way in which program and architecture work together.

We envisioned the courtyards as garden spaces, but also spaces for performance. On the interior of the building, the entry spaces—for example, there's a room that we call the *living room*—can be used for exhibitions, projections, meeting spaces, and for different kinds of performance and art. The garden courtyards could also be much more informal since there's a tradition of book sales and film screenings.

In addition to the Drawing Institute, we also designed an adjacent building that serves as the new energy house. One of the distinguishing elements about the Menil Collection is that all of the equipment that provides mechanical services is in one building; there's no stuff on the roof. It allows for a very pure profile for all of the buildings as they sit within the landscape.

One of the important things about the Drawing Institute is how one experiences the qualities of transparency and of the visual path through the building, which is often revealed through diagonal views where one enters from a corner. The courtyards and gardens play a significant role in this.

The heart of the building is the study center. It's the one place in the building where you can get close to works on paper with natural light. There are a number of different lighting scenarios that can be set up in this room and that work in concert with the conservation library, which is immediately adjacent. So drawings are moving between this suite of rooms pretty consistently.

From the west, the building feels much more like a cluster of small buildings. It's close to the scale of the surrounding residential bungalows, and the transparency of the living room is quite clear from this direction. It feels like an in-between space nested between the exhibition galleries on one side and the administrative space on the other.

The roof canopies of the courtyard were prefabricated structures, and the idea was to have a very thin roof that has a large span. They're eight inches thick and in one case span over 60 feet. There is a sense of buoyancy or levitation to them as you walk through the courtyards. All of this stretching out of the roof combined with the tree canopy in the courtyard was part of modulating the lighting that was necessary for an often-sensitive program. The roof solved a number of experiential and technical problems.

Given the sort of extreme technical and environmental controls that we had to provide for the spaces for works on paper, we felt it was critical that you always felt connected to the site around you. Oftentimes, when you're looking at works on paper in isolated rooms, you might feel totally disconnected from the environment or the larger museum. The contrast of interiority and exteriority is very present in the building. Another thing that distinguishes the Drawing Institute from most museums is that almost all of the public spaces—except for the study room—are illuminated from the side, which is more typical for houses.

STUDENT: When visiting finished projects, have you noticed how the life of the buildings reflects your intentions? Or fails to do so?

JOHNSTON: We've talked about the quality of generosity that we try to create. We try to make environments with a framework that's strong, but not so much that if you visit and the shoes are not in the right place or the table's not straight, it just falls apart. We understand that spaces sometimes take on new life and that it can be unexpected or unintentional. I wouldn't say that we're necessarily disappointed when this happens.

An example is how the courtyards are used. They're animated with kids and animals and people, and that's been really successful. Next week, I'm going back for a symposium and they're using the living room as the meeting space. I think the interiors have taken more time to adapt to a complex type of staffing and use. The administration wants to keep testing. I think the fact that the building allows them to do so speaks to the generosity of the spaces.

LEE: For me, realizations about projects always come at different moments with different buildings and it's always—at first—a very private and personal moment. Every building is slightly different. Sometimes they're topped off and you see the profile and that's when you say the building has come alive. Sometimes it's not until everything is finished, it opens and is inhabited by life that you feel it's there. With the Menil, I didn't feel it until the art was hung. When the art was hung, we realized what we had been working for. For others it will be different, but there's always a particular moment that does it for me.

BIGHAM: We talked about your collaborations with artists and you said it was perhaps less of a collaboration and more a situation where you pass it off to the artists and they respond to the work. But here, especially with the landscape, it must have been a much more traditional collaboration. The three different gardens are so effective and important. Your intention from the beginning was that they would have different characteristics and relate differently to different parts of the building. What is the communication like when you're working with the landscape architect? Are you sharing images or verbal descriptions?

JOHNSTON: All of the above. The project has been quite successful technically. It was the landscape architects, lighting consultants, and structural engineers who contributed to that. We're relying on natural conditions created by the trees as part of our light calibration. George Sexton is the lighting designer and his team built a large, accurately-scaled model. It was as long as the two conference tables we're sitting at now. Michael van Valkenburgh's landscape team took light level readings and built very accurate models of trees relative to what we were planning.

We were using all of that information to help us refine the shape and placement of the landscape and the shape of the roof.

Michael van Valkenburgh, who is working on huge master plans all over the country, was fascinated with the idea of making gardens here. Again, it was almost like going back to a domestic scale. He immediately jumped at the idea of these garden rooms and his office had a sense of how they could be different in a way that would speak to the environment of Houston and their directionality, scale, and relationship to the building. Michael was thinking as much about shading as he was about planting in terms of the relationship to works on paper and the poetics of lines on paper. These contributions end up being a really import-ant part of what you experience when you're there. The solution was as much about foliage as it was about light and shadow in the courtyards.

STUDENT: Can you describe working with clients a bit more and how you develop ideas along the way?

JOHNSTON: A really good example of development is working through mockups. It's just so important. We did material mockups, wall assembly mockups, all sorts of models of different parts at different scales. We basically built this building in small pieces and then rebuilt it a final time. Not every project budget or schedule or client can accommodate doing this, but the more we practice, the more we insist on it. Because if you're going to do this kind of research and experimentation with materials and assemblies, you can't guess. You have to test it. It takes a level of commitment on everyone's part to get that right.

LEE: So many stars have to line up. We were recommended for consideration and the Menil visited us, so we developed a rapport with the director. Then we were invited to do the competition, and there were some very well-known and well-regarded offices competing with us. Often, you'll see a younger office or local office invited to a competition as a token gesture. We were probably that younger, smaller office. For them to pick the scheme and architect that they thought were right for them takes a certain confidence.

There's an ethos about how the Menil works with artists and acquires work, which is to always try to invest in artists that are early in their career. I think the board and the director has carried that on even after the founders passed. We saw this as an opportunity for us also to learn about the history of the collection and the campus.

UCLA Margo Leavin Graduate Art Studios sculpture yard

Before we started any design work, we spent a few weeks just studying the evolution of the foundation within that part of Houston. When we presented at the competition, we talked for half an hour about the history of the site. After the presentation, some people that had worked there for years came up to us and said they had learned a lot about the history of the place. So we put in a lot of work just understanding the context of things and in return, they really treated us as artists. That's something quite unique in the whole experience of the six or seven years working on that project.

The last project we want to discuss is the Margo Leavin UCLA Graduate Art Studios. It's not on the UCLA campus; it's on a satellite campus in an industrial area called the Hayden Tract in Culver City in midtown L.A. Culver City is an area that was known for film production. In the middle of the century, there were a lot of these industrial warehouses that started off as manufacturing buildings. Later on they became post-production spaces. UCLA had owned the building since the early 80s, but it was falling apart. We were commissioned to renovate it and add on to it. It was an old wallpaper factory with three barrel-vault truss roofs. Over time, other buildings and components had been added around and onto it. The main building is raised three feet off the ground for loading and unloading, but all the other add-ons are not, so in between the edges of the building, there are all these stairs and ramps that create a lot of transitions to get around.

There has been a lot of gentrification in and around the area and one thing that the clients wanted was to preserve the industrial roughness of the warehouse. We had many meetings with the city, the faculty, and the students. The students in particular were insistent on maintaining the roughness of the building because of

UCLA Margo Leavin Graduate Art Studios main entry

all the other trendy and avant-garde stuff going up. They said, "We want this building to be rough. We want to be able to throw trash in that corner." [laughter] So everything is exposed: HVAC, electrical, etcetera. Things are left fairly raw in a number of ways.

The first thing we did was to get rid of all of the buildings and add-ons that had collected like barnacles. The second thing we did was we added a new L-shaped floor that is raised three feet and wraps the old warehouse. Everything becomes one level with the rest of the building. The third thing we did was to decide that we didn't want to *design* it at all; we just wanted to take the warehouse construction and proliferate it around the whole thing as a new wall. In the end, we created a new form of barrel vault roof that is very similar to the wood barrel vault roof that was already there and it covers the whole site. Over time, the program began to evolve to include a type of buffer zone or buffer space similar to what we did at the Green Line Art Center and the Menil. There are spaces that are covered but not conditioned; there are rooms that exist between the interior and exterior. These become the sculp-

ture yard, gardens, courtyards, and so on. The exterior surface is tilt-up construction: a series of pillowed surfaces that blend in with the columns and structure of the warehouse.

BIGHAM: The pillows have similar scalloping to UIC. Which came first, the UIC project or this?

LEE: This project came first.

STUDENT: This scalloping is from the Chile house, too, right?

JOHNSTON: Similar surface. It's not disconnected, but we got there from a different starting point.

BIGHAM: It's interesting that it's solid here. At UIC, the same form is porous. It's a change of materiality and a change of effect.

JOHNSTON: The solidness here helped with faster construction— it's a much simpler process. We're also very mindful that it can get hot in L.A. The concrete here acts almost like an adobe wall in that it's absorbing heat for a large part of the day.

It's also worth noting again that the courtyards weren't part of the brief. We were thinking about the problems posed by light and daylighting. These spaces emerged as something that could help us in terms of the urban campus spaces we were dealing with, but they could also help with more technical lighting issues. It added cost to the project, but it was one of those moments where there are parts of the building where we came in under budget, so we could afford to have those courtyards and gardens. In the end, they would become the defining attribute of the building.

LEE: The planning of the studio spaces is somewhere between a grid and a labyrinth. There are all these little cul-de-sacs like a little city. Sometimes you walk into one of these cul-de-sacs and it may have the entrances to five or six studios in such a way that it forms a local neighborhood. But even the walls of the studios are only finished up to a certain height. The studs are exposed; you can hear the neighbors. This all adds to the roughness of the space and the community made by the students.

STUDENT: Do you find it hard to convince clients to go for the extra-programmatic things that aren't in the original brief? Even when you're under budget elsewhere?

JOHNSTON: Sometimes, but generally our approach is to create the right tools to help them make a decision. So maybe it's giving them really high quality and polished models to show what we're talking about. Maybe it's about providing technical data that justifies an idea. Or, as in the case of the Menil, doing a deep dive into history and understanding that the courtyard was a critical part of the residence and a part of the museum, and that it should be part of the Drawing Institute too. A good enough argument will make it seem like something was just missing from the program brief.

STUDENT: I'm interested in the idea of spanning because so many of these projects are about organizing individual moments or rooms under a collective umbrella. So as much as there is a unifying idea or framework, there's an equal focus on the character and specificity of the individual room.

LEE: I think it comes from Louis Kahn, for whom the individual module of the room was very important. For many of our projects, the delineation of boundary is very important. I think Kahn himself had to make a decision when everyone else was working on the breaking of boundaries. For a moment, everything was about one

space leaking into another. Everything was about making architecture lighter. And Kahn decided that he wanted a more defined room. Aldo Rossi had to make that decision also. For us, when we started practicing, everyone was about breaking boundaries. Everything was about folding. There's space for those movements, but we thought that this type of thinking—about boundary and room and clear delineation—was missing. Then the scale of the work starts to grow and we start moving from single objects to agglomerations and collections.

JOHNSTON: Scale alone will challenge us again. Many of these projects are 50,000 or 75,000 square feet—it's big but it's not like a 300,000 square-foot space. There's still a quality of roominess and I think the connection back to the typology of the house and that sort of intimacy will always be important. It keeps getting tested as we have different programs to wrestle with.

STUDENT: I have a question about working with the existing context. For example, here you added the L-shaped part between existing elements. What criteria do you use to establish the priorities in making design decisions? Client? History? Budget?

JOHNSTON: It's different all the time, but a lot of our work involves trying come up with things that can solve multiple problems. It's rarely about just one input or factor. We often hear about solutions being holistic responses, but the challenges are holistic as well. Very rarely is any issue exclusive to itself when it comes to architecture.

STUDENT: When you talk about the early practice and what was going on in the discipline—when everything was about folding, for example—you say that you were trying to understand things from a different perspective. Jackson Pollack's drip technique was a liberating mechanism that became a form-making mechanism later on, for both himself and others. Do you have explicit conversations about these things and their possible paths to becoming form-making tools? How do you keep up on all of the developments in both architecture and other fields?

LEE: Architecture is different than the other disciplines and we don't have any anxiety about needing to be on the very front lines like that. There are other offices that jump on the newest gadgets and tools and that's okay. Being able to examine things as they develop gives us some critical distance. There's also a lot to do with precedents. How do you define precedents? What do you measure up against? Do you measure up against history or do you measure up against something else that is going on around the world? Cultivating knowledge—and it could be almost anything—is very important. We try to always grow with respect to our interests and knowledge; we're always learning. When we look at Kahn, and then at Stirling, it begins to form a network of relationships and differences. And then you just keep going deeper. It can begin as something superficial, but it's important for us to always go deeper into it and to understand who did it, where it's from, and why. Architecture should not be a monoculture. The world is made of relationships and reactions and histories. In the U.S. it's a little harder to build projects that you don't have experience with for a number of reasons. But you have to do what you can to cultivate knowledge. Hopefully, that becomes an opportunity to build.

BIGHAM: If you look at the various European models of architectural education, when students graduate they are either licensed or in some other way fed directly into a political or social system that encourages young risk-taking architects to build public buildings. In the U.S. we don't have anything like this.

LEE: This is the first thing I realized at my first teaching job in Europe. I was at the ETH Zurich, which has an incredible reputation as a university. People were approaching me to do buildings because of my affiliation with the ETH. We came back to the U.S. and I was teaching at UCLA and that alone wasn't enough; we had to prove that we could build, despite being related to the university. There's a chasm between academia and practice here. No one person can solve it, but it's an issue that needs to be addressed.

Most of the buildings that you see as you drive home represent what 99% of architecture is like and it's getting worse and worse. In the universities, we're fighting for this 1%, and it often feels like it's not going to change. I'm concerned that architecture is becoming a niche sport and that it's getting harder and harder to engage in the construction of the built environment.

BIGHAM: It does seem like many in my generation have leaned into academia because there simply wasn't an economic model to practice given the hesitancy of clients or institutions to take risks.

JOHNSTON: When we curated our biennial, there were a number of younger architects whose aspiration wasn't actually to build buildings, but to intensely work on other elements of the city. People are working with artists and doing interventions. They're really trying to be professionals and to problem solve at the scale of architecture, but they don't really want to go work at a corporate office. There's so much interest there, but the risk averse culture of building in the U.S. sets up a real hierarchy of who can participate and who cannot. For academics, self-generating your own projects or doing installation-based work is one model that can work.

STUDENT: Is there a danger of becoming too insular or inverted though? It seems like academia can be an internal loop where there's no chance for those outside of it to understand the issues that happen within.

LEE: I think it should absolutely not be autonomous. There are moments in history where things become too autonomous and need adjustment. There are moments where we spread out too thin and lose a core base of knowledge or context. Based on the last 10 years, I would say that architecture needs to reexamine its core. There's been so much talk about interdisciplinary work and a need to be interdisciplinary, but you have to be very good at what you are and what you do so that when you come together with other fields you can contribute. The interdisciplinary idea should not be an excuse for dilettantism. This is what I'm passionate about in terms of the discipline right now.

STUDENT: How do you overlap all of these ideas and agendas with the individual studios that you teach?

LEE: I think it's always implicit in how we work in the office and how we work with students but it's probably not that explicit in the studio brief. I think that sometimes instruction at schools is overtly wild and free because we think, hey, students don't have the burdens of the real world. But I don't think this is the right way to do it. I think that understanding constraints is the springboard for creativity. For me, I'm not looking for spectacular or gymnastic buildings in studio; I'm looking for really thoughtful and well-considered ideas. I'm curious about this building, Knowlton Hall. You all study here and work here. What is it about this building that interests you?

STUDENT: For me, it's all about how light and shadows play on surfaces. But it's more than a building; it's an environment and a place unto itself. It's like an aircraft carrier at sea. You can feel the difference in temperature over the seasons, not just in the air but in the walls. The raw concrete walls are more than just walls, though. They define a series of spaces that feel almost urban in scale, with primary thoroughfares and back alleys. I think the moments of openness contribute to that. There's a problem with spray painting, though. [laughter]

JOHNSTON: It seems like a space that is animated based on how people use it, whether it's a classroom or a gallery or a studio;

there's a lot of change that happens through how it's occupied. And it seems like the building isn't super prescriptive about that. Again, it's the idea of generosity that we try to embellish our projects with.

LEE: Do you think this building works better as a sequence or as a collection of individual moments? Do you like the interior as much as the exterior?

BIGHAM: The sequence is something that's really grown on me over the last year. As a visitor, circulation is initially quite atypical and complicated. There's no single way to get from point A to point B, so you're never sure about what staircase is going to get you there. But by the time you begin to understand and know the building, it's hard to imagine doing it any other way. From the student point of view is it the same?

STUDENT: Yeah. I like the moments and sequences. I think of the interior as very sequential, mostly driven by the ramp and the deep views into spaces. I think of the exterior as a collection of discrete moments, with the courtyards, the oculus, the edges of the site, and the marble shingles. I think it takes time. I walk a lot of people through the building on visits and there are often comments about things being confusing or unfocused. A lot of times the lack of initial clarity is interpreted as a bad experience.

JOHNSTON: We talk about this kind of quality often. We talk about a way of perceiving something that, instead of looking at something as spectacular and being wowed, is almost better if at first you can't quite understand it and that over time your connection deepens. That's poetry and storytelling in architecture: where the building unfolds and grows on you as you read it and experience it. I think that's the kind of work that we aspire to.

LEE: Jeff Koons talks about how every work needs to have something that you're attracted to for five seconds. And then after you attract me for five seconds, there should be something that will make me stay for five minutes. Sometimes you have the five-minute moment that works, but you don't have the first five seconds. Sometimes you certainly have the five seconds of seduction, but then the interest is gone. The question is, can the five-second element be so pleasing that it could be slightly estranged and veiled as something that maybe prompts individuals to find out more about the whole sequencing? With this building, I have to say that I had to take five turns to get to the men's room. [laughter] So I got a little lost at first, but now I'm intrigued by the rest of it and the longer experiences of really knowing the building.

STUDENT: As the practice matures, how are you managing the office and the projects? Are you resisting becoming a larger office where projects just go out with a name on them but not necessarily the attention of the founders and principals? Do you do more curation of projects within the office versus hands-on design?

LEE: Again, as the office grows, other people begin to take on responsibilities. In the beginning we did everything. At some point, you realize you need to shift from being a designer to being a critic and manager. Sometimes we set a direction and sometimes it's more of a team-based discovery or development. But the process is always open to evolution and ideas; that's why you have a studio of people that you want to work with. It's kind of like going from operating as a chef to operating as a restauranteur.

JOHNSTON: I also think that we've expanded the traditional trajectory of going straight into being architects who are building buildings. By doing curatorial work and having leadership positions at schools, we've attracted different kinds of clients. In a way, our client base is narrower than if we were just doing 50 buildings, and that's both good and bad. This has expanded our engagement with the discipline more broadly and, in terms of producing buildings, it has fostered a smaller community. But I think our clients are willing to go deep with us, and that's the kind of office we are. We've made the bed and we're lying in it. We've been very fortunate to be able to work with the people we've worked with. We continue to be mindful of that.

MENIL DRAWING INSTITUTE

HOUSTON, TEXAS (2018)

Aerial of the MDI and Menil campus

The Menil Drawing Institute (MDI) is sited within the 30 acre campus of The Menil Collection. Positioned in the geographic center of the campus, the MDI is adjacent to the Cy Twombly Pavilion and nested among the historic bungalows that make up the fabric of this neighborhood of art. The design of the MDI honors the legacy of intimacy and direct engagement with art that underlies the domestic and institutional character of the Menil campus. Situated in a park-like setting, the new building assumes the scale of both a house and a museum, with a low-lying, elongated profile that blends with the architecture of the historic campus while signaling a new dimension for future growth.

MDI model

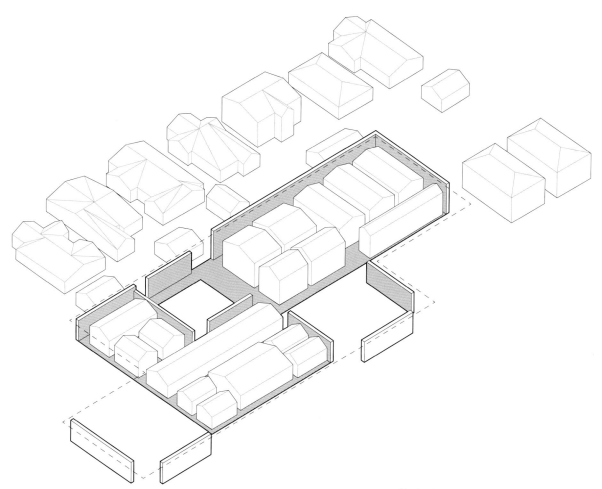

Massing diagram of interior domestic-scaled museum spaces

South elevation

East courtyard

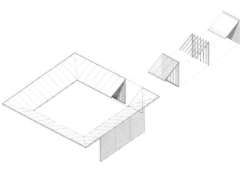

Axonometric detail of steel plate roof construction

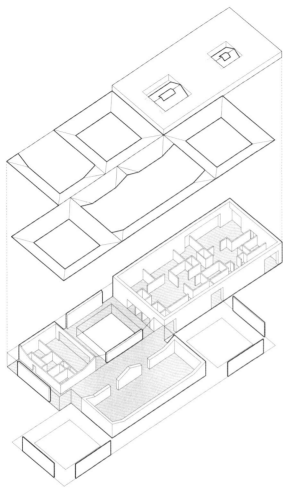

The MDI is composed of a series of buildings and courtyards unified by a white steel plate roof that hovers over the landscape. The roof defines two entry courtyards to the east and west. A third courtyard within the building links public and private zones of the building and organizes circulation between offices and scholar study areas. These courtyards belong to both the park and the building as thresholds between outdoor and indoor spaces. Within the courtyards, the underlying folds of the roof plane embrace the tree canopies to create a shaded atmosphere around the building. Shedding light, the roof reflects the shadows of the trees and contrasts with the deep grey cedar planks that clad the building.

Axonometric of roof geometry
(gables and dormers are pitched to calibrate light and scale)

South porch

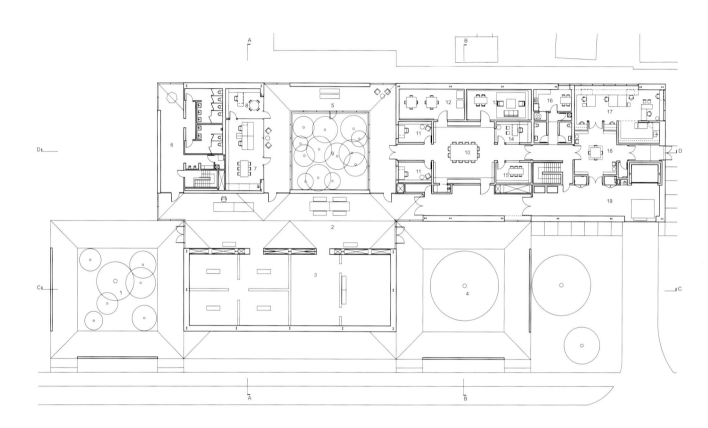

FIRST FLOOR PLAN

1. ENTRY COURTYARD
2. LIVING ROOM
3. GALLERY
4. EAST COURTYARD
5. CLOISTER
6. ANNEX
7. OFFICE
8. CHIEF CURATOR

9. SCHOLAR COURTYARD
10. DRAWING ROOM
11. SCHOLAR OFFICE
12. SALON
13. COLLECTOR ROOM
14. PROCTOR ROOM
15. SEMINAR ROOM
16. BREAKROOM

17. CONSERVATOR LAB
18. LIBRARY ATRIUM
19. LOADING

FT
0   10   40

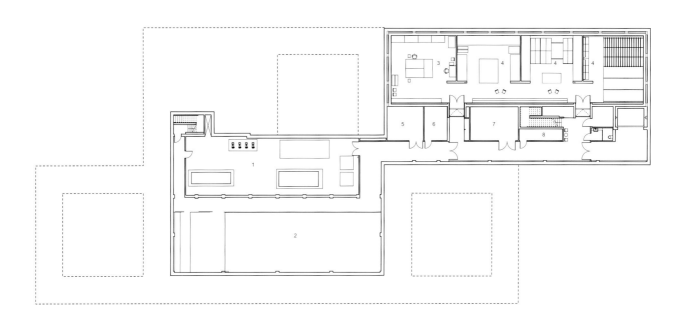

BASEMENT

1. MECHANICAL
2. NON-ART STORAGE
3. MATTING - PHOTO
4. ART STORAGE
5. ELECTRICAL
6. AV/IT
7. HOLDING ROOM
8. SECURITY

FT
0   10   40

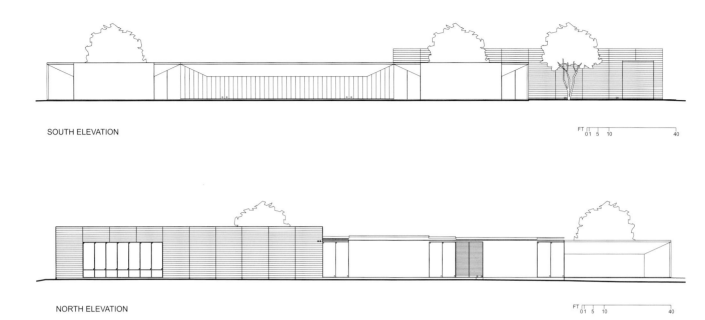

SOUTH ELEVATION

FT
0 1 5 10   40

NORTH ELEVATION

FT
0 1 5 10   40

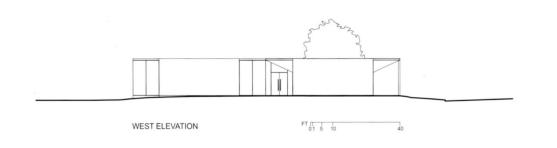

WEST ELEVATION

FT
0 1 5 10   40

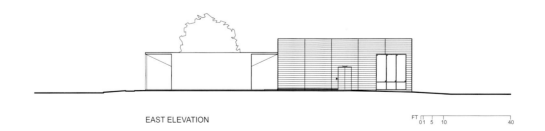

EAST ELEVATION

FT
0 1 5 10   40

West entry and courtyard

West courtyard

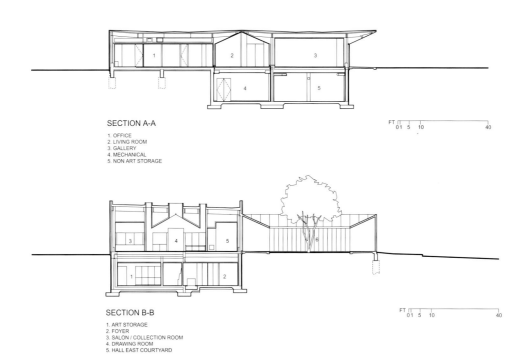

SECTION A-A

1. OFFICE
2. LIVING ROOM
3. GALLERY
4. MECHANICAL
5. NON ART STORAGE

FT | 0 1 5   10 | 40

SECTION B-B

1. ART STORAGE
2. FOYER
3. SALON / COLLECTION ROOM
4. DRAWING ROOM
5. HALL EAST COURTYARD

FT | 0 1 5   10 | 40

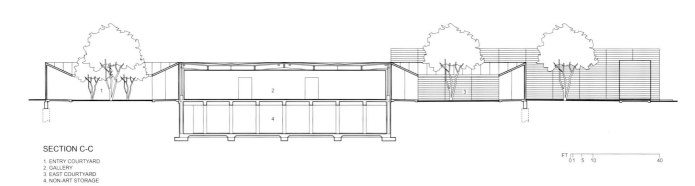

SECTION C-C

1. ENTRY COURTYARD
2. GALLERY
3. EAST COURTYARD
4. NON-ART STORAGE

FT | 0 1 5   10 | 40

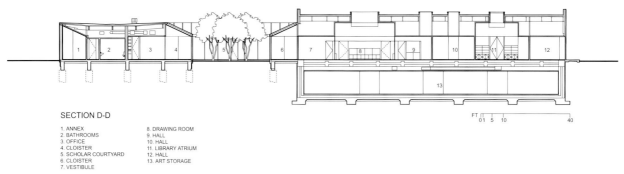

SECTION D-D

1. ANNEX
2. BATHROOMS
3. OFFICE
4. CLOISTER
5. SCHOLAR COURTYARD
6. CLOISTER
7. VESTIBULE
8. DRAWING ROOM
9. HALL
10. HALL
11. LIBRARY ATRIUM
12. HALL
13. ART STORAGE

FT | 0 1 5   10 | 40

Scholar courtyard

Entry living room

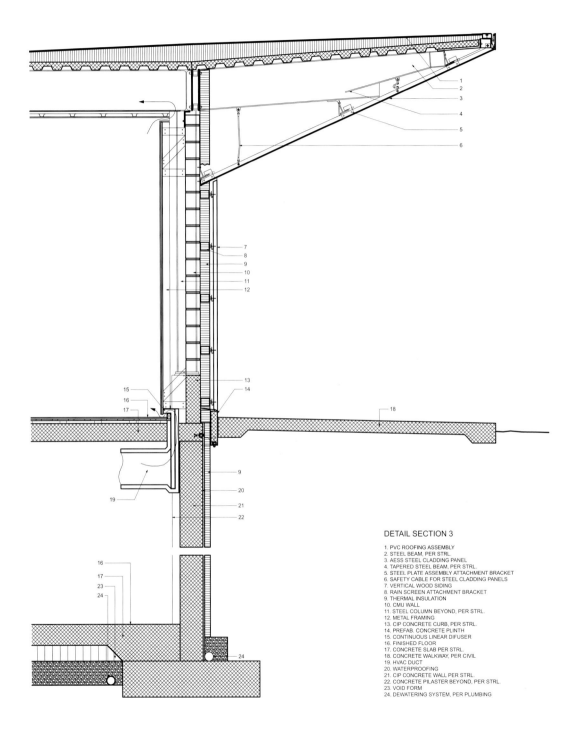

DETAIL SECTION 3

1. PVC ROOFING ASSEMBLY
2. STEEL BEAM, PER STRL.
3. AESS STEEL CLADDING PANEL
4. TAPERED STEEL BEAM, PER STRL.
5. STEEL PLATE ASSEMBLY ATTACHMENT BRACKET
6. SAFETY CABLE FOR STEEL CLADDING PANELS
7. VERTICAL WOOD SIDING
8. RAIN SCREEN ATTACHMENT BRACKET
9. THERMAL INSULATION
10. CMU WALL
11. STEEL COLUMN BEYOND, PER STRL.
12. METAL FRAMING
13. CIP CONCRETE CURB, PER STRL.
14. PREFAB. CONCRETE PLINTH
15. CONTINUOUS LINEAR DIFUSER
16. FINISHED FLOOR
17. CONCRETE SLAB PER STRL.
18. CONCRETE WALKWAY, PER CIVIL
19. HVAC DUCT
20. WATERPROOFING
21. CIP CONCRETE WALL PER STRL.
22. CONCRETE PILASTER BEYOND, PER STRL.
23. VOID FORM
24. DEWATERING SYSTEM, PER PLUMBING

South porch

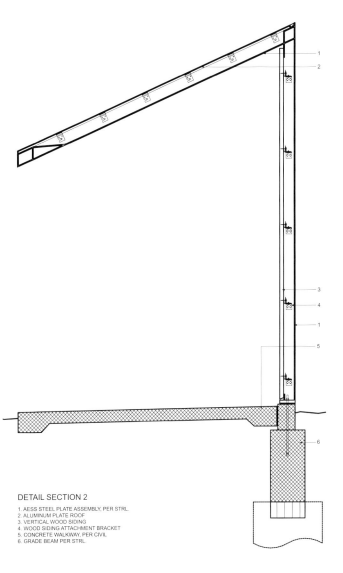

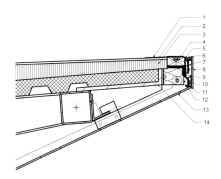

DETAIL SECTION 2

1. AESS STEEL PLATE ASSEMBLY, PER STRL.
2. ALUMINUM PLATE ROOF
3. VERTICAL WOOD SIDING
4. WOOD SIDING ATTACHMENT BRACKET
5. CONCRETE WALKWAY, PER CIVIL
6. GRADE BEAM PER STRL.

DETAIL - ROOF EDGE

1. PVC ROOFING MEMBRANE
2. ROOF COVER BOARD
3. ROOF INSULATION
4. NAILER
5. CONTINUOUS CLEAT
6. PVC COATED METAL FLASHING
7. STEEL ANGLE, SPACING AS REQ.
8. AESS STEEL CLADDING FASCIA
9. CONTINUOUS CUSTOM STEEL ANGLE
10. HT SELF ADHERING SHEET FLASHING
11. Z-CLIP, SPACING AS REQ.
12. FABRICATED STANDOFF TO SUPPORT ROOF EDGE ASSEMBLY
13. AESS STEEL CLADDING PANEL W/ HIGH PERFORMANCE STEEL COATING
14. CONTINUOUS BENT PLATE, PER STRL.

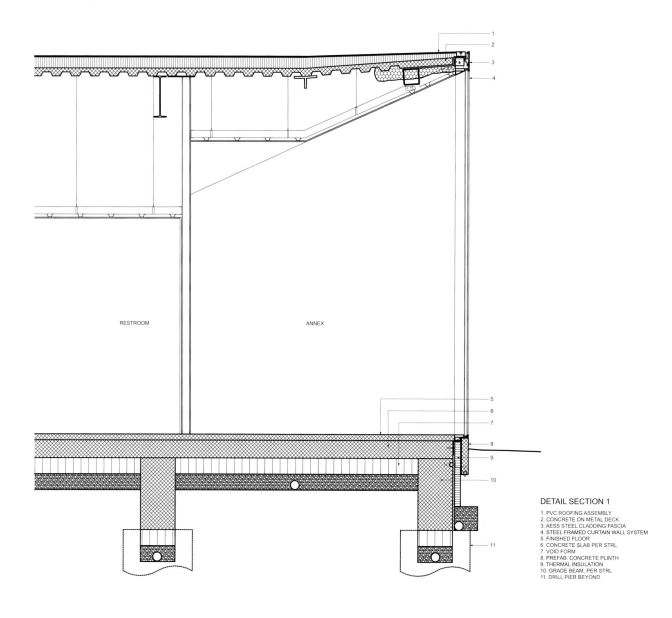

RESTROOM

ANNEX

DETAIL SECTION 1

1. PVC ROOFING ASSEMBLY
2. CONCRETE ON METAL DECK
3. AESS STEEL CLADDING FASCIA
4. STEEL FRAMED CURTAIN WALL SYSTEM
5. FINISHED FLOOR
6. CONCRETE SLAB PER STRL.
7. VOID FORM
8. PREFAB. CONCRETE PLINTH
9. THERMAL INSULATION
10. GRADE BEAM, PER STRL
11. DRILL PIER BEYOND

Annex and west courtyard

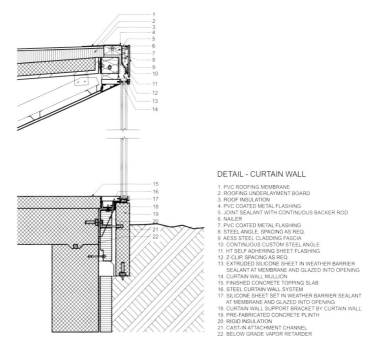

DETAIL - CURTAIN WALL

1. PVC ROOFING MEMBRANE
2. ROOFING UNDERLAYMENT BOARD
3. ROOF INSULATION
4. PVC COATED METAL FLASHING
5. JOINT SEALANT WITH CONTINUOUS BACKER ROD
6. NAILER
7. PVC COATED METAL FLASHING
8. STEEL ANGLE, SPACING AS REQ.
9. AESS STEEL CLADDING FASCIA
10. CONTINUOUS CUSTOM STEEL ANGLE
11. HT SELF ADHERING SHEET FLASHING
12. Z-CLIP, SPACING AS REQ.
13. EXTRUDED SILICONE SHEET IN WEATHER BARRIER
    SEALANT AT MEMBRANE AND GLAZED INTO OPENING
14. CURTAIN WALL MULLION
15. FINISHED CONCRETE TOPPING SLAB
16. STEEL CURTAIN WALL SYSTEM
17. SILICONE SHEET SET IN WEATHER BARRIER SEALANT
    AT MEMBRANE AND GLAZED INTO OPENING
18. CURTAIN WALL SUPPORT BRACKET BY CURTAIN WALL
19. PRE-FABRICATED CONCRETE PLINTH
20. RIGID INSULATION
21. CAST-IN ATTACHMENT CHANNEL
22. BELOW GRADE VAPOR RETARDER

UCLA MARGO LEAVIN GRADUATE ART STUDIOS

CULVER CITY, CALIFORNIA (2019)

Above and left: Aerial of existing UCLA Graduate Arts complex within the Hayden Tract

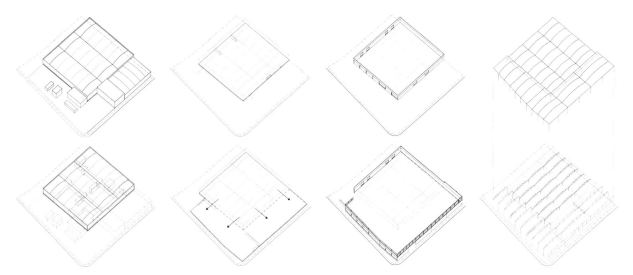

Four step strategy: purge the obsolete; extend ground; tilt-up facade; expand roof

The UCLA Graduate Art Studios restore and expand portions of the existing Culver City campus that have been located in the industrial Hayden Tract since 1986. The 48,000-square-foot building includes the adaptive reuse of a 20,000-square-foot historic wallpaper factory, which is converted into a neighborhood of graduate art studios. A new 28,000-square-foot structure will accommodate laboratories, galleries, classrooms, and an artist-in-residence loft for the six disciplines of ceramics, interdisciplinary studio, new genres, painting and drawing, photography, and sculpture. The new complex fuses together the new and old structures to allow for differentiation and complexity of use.

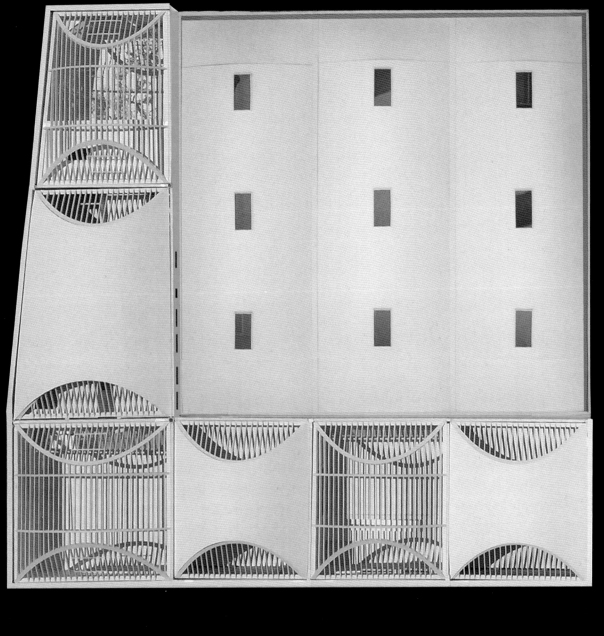
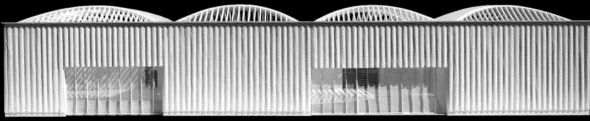

NORTH ELEVATION

FT ⊩ ┬ ┬ ┬ ┬
    01 5 10   40

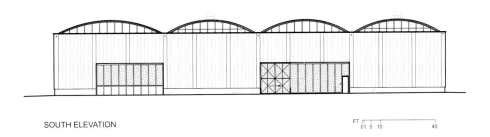

SOUTH ELEVATION

FT ⊩ ┬ ┬ ┬ ┬
    01 5 10   40

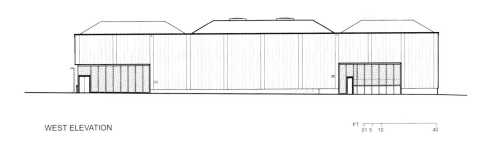

WEST ELEVATION

FT ⊩ ┬ ┬ ┬ ┬
    01 5 10   40

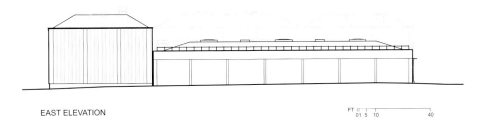

EAST ELEVATION

FT ⊩ ┬ ┬ ┬ ┬
    01 5 10   40

Opposite: Aerial and south addition

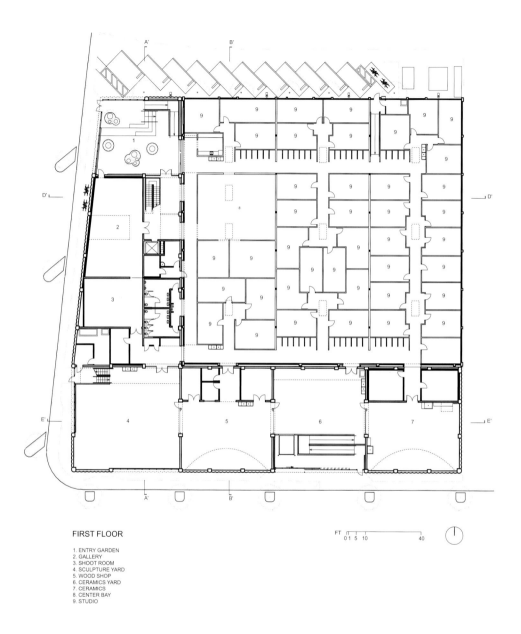

FIRST FLOOR

1. ENTRY GARDEN
2. GALLERY
3. SHOOT ROOM
4. SCULPTURE YARD
5. WOOD SHOP
6. CERAMICS YARD
7. CERAMICS
8. CENTER BAY
9. STUDIO

FT
0 1 5 10   40

The internal organization of the restored warehouse is conceived like a small city. Individual artist studios—the basic dwelling unit of the city—are clustered to form a collection of blocks within the existing warehouse, without delineating zones according to discipline. Circulation areas are defined by niches for material storage, cul-de-sacs for shared entries and infrastructure, and collective spaces for class critiques. The material palette of the building supports the need for raw and undifferentiated space and function.

The pillowed profile of the tilt-up concrete facade optimizes the thickness of the material for thermal efficiency, eliminating additional layers of insulation and waterproofing. The scalloped facade is animated by light and shadow, but stripped of any details to mark its identity or function. On the interior, minimal finishing and cladding present a potent, yet unfinished, material landscape suitable for artists' studios.

Visualization of the new addition

Interior street connecting individual artist studios

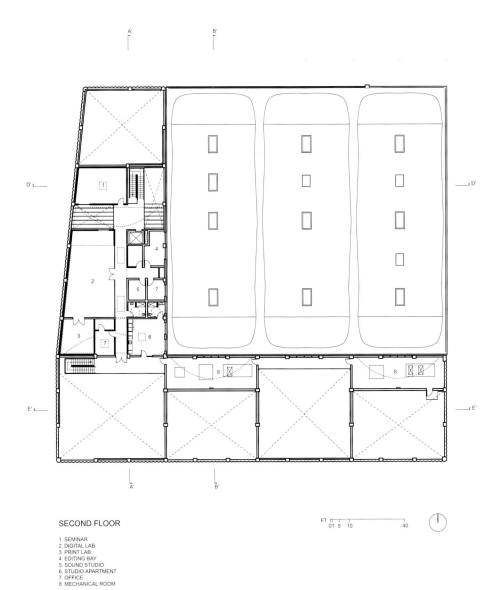

SECOND FLOOR

1. SEMINAR
2. DIGITAL LAB
3. PRINT LAB
4. EDITING BAY
5. SOUND STUDIO
6. STUDIO APARTMENT
7. OFFICE
8. MECHANICAL ROOM

FT
01 5 10   40

Surrounding the warehouse, the shared programs of labs and classrooms are positioned
between double-height, multi-functional yards—all of which are sheltered by a continuous vaulted roof structure. Formed by curved glulam beams and clad in a combination
of roofing membranes and translucent glazed panels, the roof recalls the historic bow
truss structure of the warehouse with a new scale and structural dimension. While the
studios, gallery, and workshops are spaces of specific use, the indoor-outdoor yards are
undetermined in terms of form, program, and atmosphere to support the unexpected, fluid uses of production, installation, and exhibition. The entry yard on the northwest corner
of the building, organized around a grove of ponytail palms, is both a meeting space and
communal garden.

Sculpture courtyard facing north

Cantilevered entry courtyard

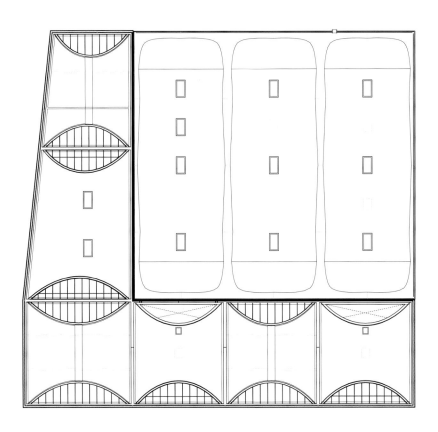

ROOF

FT
01 5 10   40

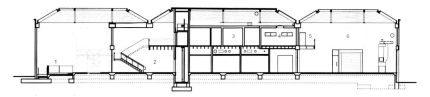

SECTION A-A'

1. ENTRY GARDEN
2. ENTRY
3. SOUND STUDIO
4. STUDIO APARTMENT
5. EXTERIOR MEZZANINE
6. SCULPTURE YARD

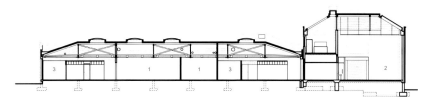

SECTION B-B'

1. CENTER BAY
2. WOOD SHOP
3. STUDIO

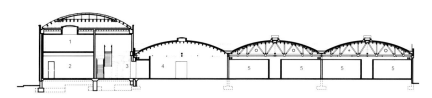

SECTION C-C'

1. SEMINAR
2. GALLERY
3. ENTRY
4. CENTER
5. STUDIO

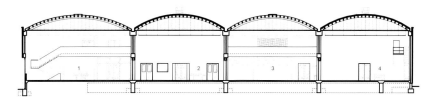

SECTION D-D'

1. SCULPTURE YARD
2. WOOD SHOP
3. CERAMICS
4. CERAMICS YARD

CHICAGO, ILLINOIS (2019)

Aerial view

The historic Walter Netsch campus at the University of Illinois at Chicago was conceived as an adaptable architectural network; interconnected communal and social spaces were intended to facilitate learning and sharing and unify buildings across the campus. The new UIC Center for the Arts advances these original architectural aspirations in a contemporary building, presenting an opportunity to showcase the important role of the arts in the university through an iconic and highly functional building that serves the campus and the city. This building will realize aspects of Netsch's vision for Project Y, which intended to combine a public concert hall, theater, and cultural spaces to create, in Netsch's words, "the Lincoln Center of Chicago."

In the unique setting of Harrison Field and the adjacent expressways—currently experienced as voids in the urban fabric—the new arts building connects the campus to the city through transit and pedestrian routes. Two stepped, geometric towers form a highly visible gateway to the campus and house the theater in the tower to the east and the concert hall to the west. The western tower steps as a traditional ziggurat; the eastern tower grows in size as it ascends, declaring its presence to downtown Chicago. During the day, the towers reflect light and veil interior activity through a layer of curved and perforated metal panels encasing the glass curtain wall. At night, the veil appears to recede with interior illumination that reveals the brightly colored performance halls within.

View of the towers from the expressway

Connecting the towers is a plateau: a sprawling and voluminous space activated by informal performances, rehearsals, arts exhibitions, and campus life where students and the public meet. The plateau establishes a new built horizon that anchors the Center for the Arts to Harrison Field, offering multiple points of entry from paths across the campus and the city. At the cross section of Harrison and Halsted streets, it supports the symmetrical objects of theater and concert hall above like two vases on a table—defining a building in the round without a true front or back. Between these arts spaces is the winter garden. The structural frame of the winter garden roof spans across the plateau to connect the two large performance halls. With its full glass roof, the winter garden will be a communal hub for students and faculty on the north side of the UIC campus, at the heart of the College of Architecture, Design, and the Arts.

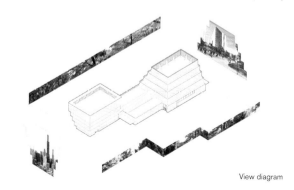

View diagram

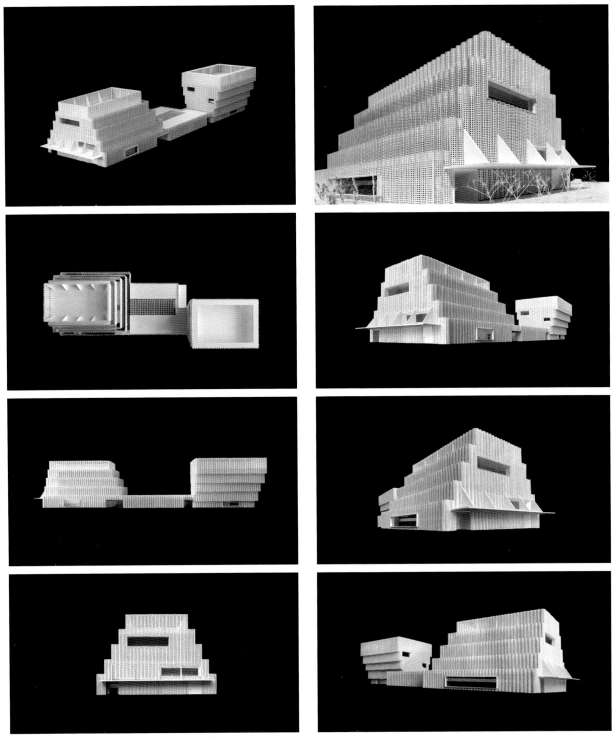

Model views

View of towers from the north

West elevaiton of concert hall

Entrance

Atrium

Interior street

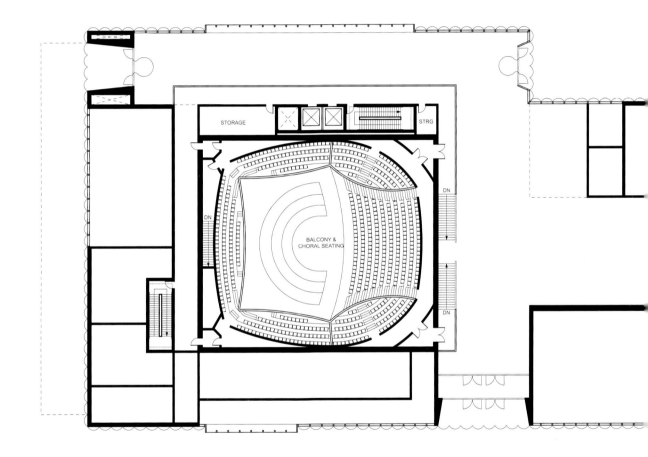

LEVEL 1.5 FLOOR PLAN

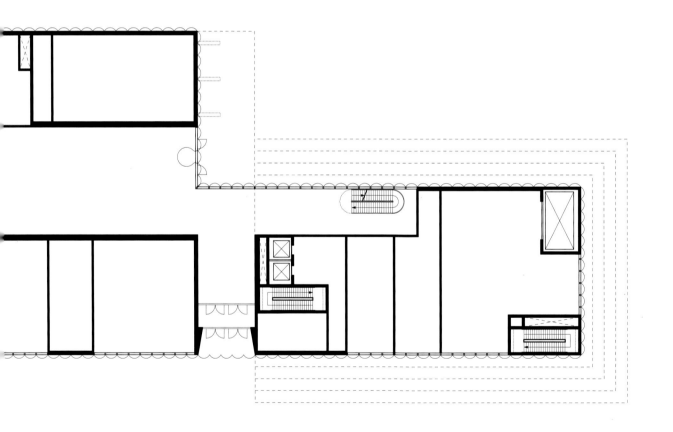

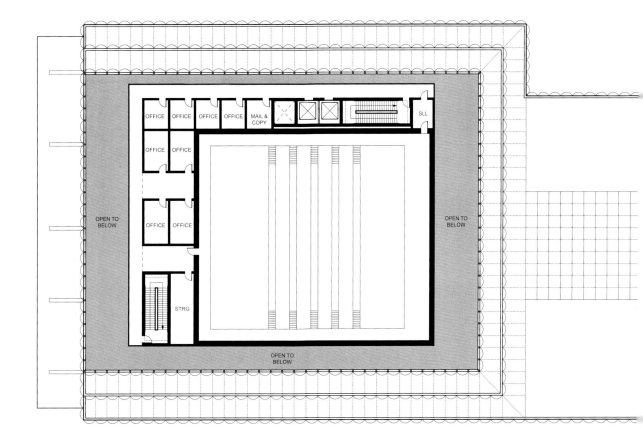

OFFICE   OFFICE   OFFICE   OFFICE   MAIL &
                                    COPY

OFFICE   OFFICE

OPEN TO
BELOW

OFFICE   OFFICE

STRG

OPEN TO
BELOW

SLL

OPEN TO
BELOW

LEVEL 3 FLOOR PLAN

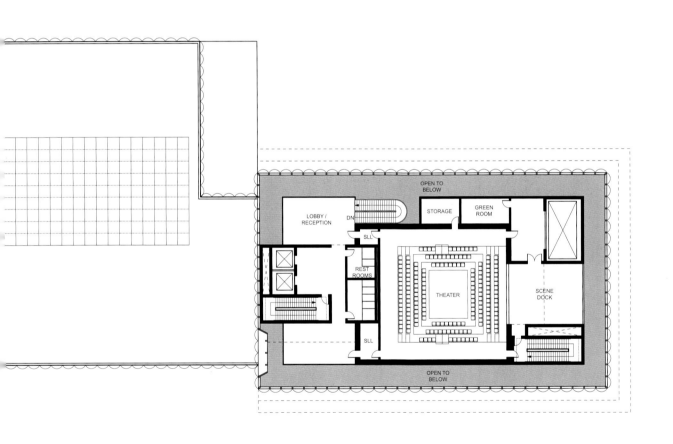

OPEN TO
BELOW

LOBBY /
RECEPTION

DN

STORAGE

GREEN
ROOM

SLL

REST
ROOMS

THEATER

SCENE
DOCK

SLL

OPEN TO
BELOW

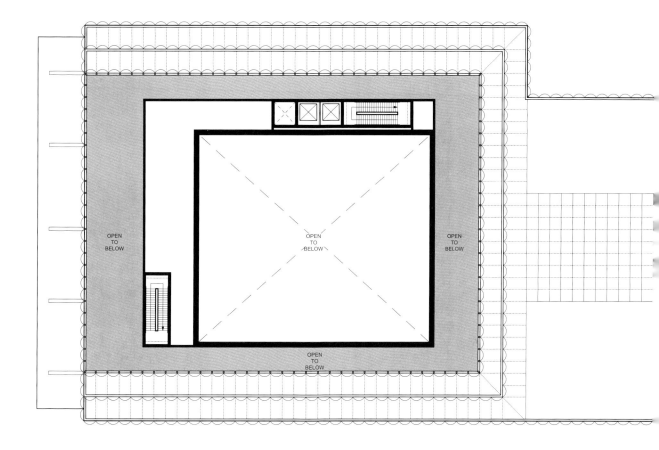

OPEN
TO
BELOW

OPEN
TO
BELOW

OPEN
TO
BELOW

OPEN
TO
BELOW

LEVEL 3.5 FLOOR PLAN

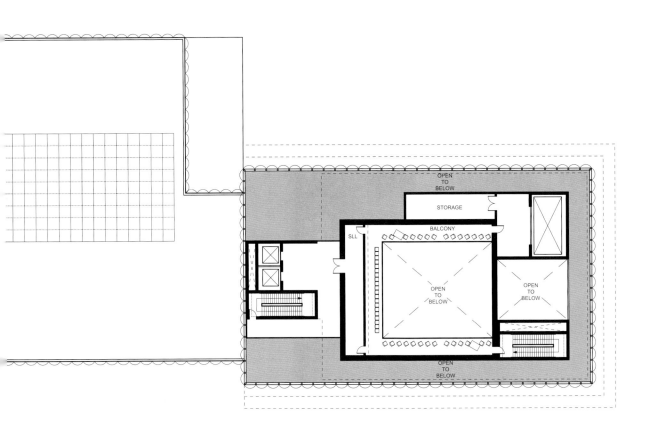

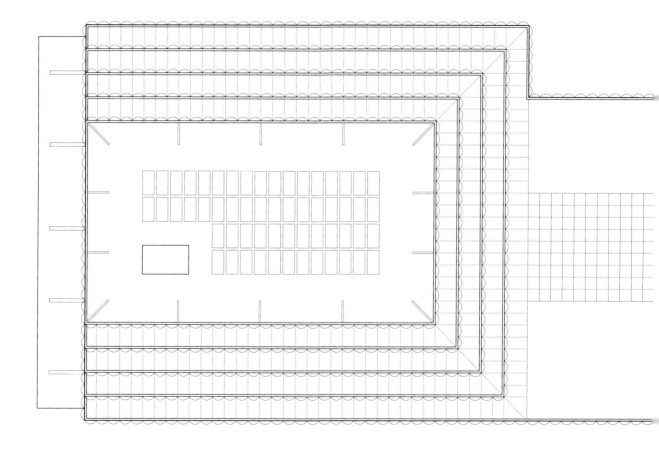

ROOF PLAN

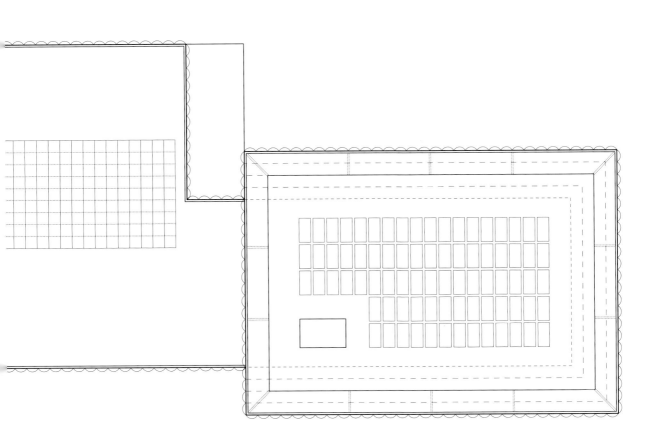

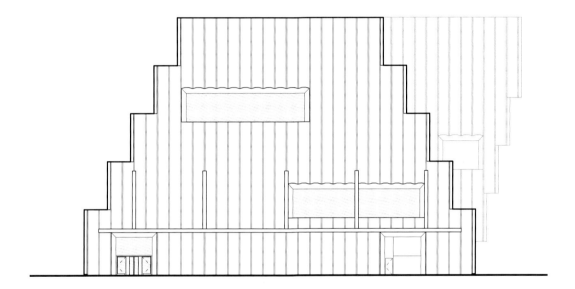

WEST ELEVATION

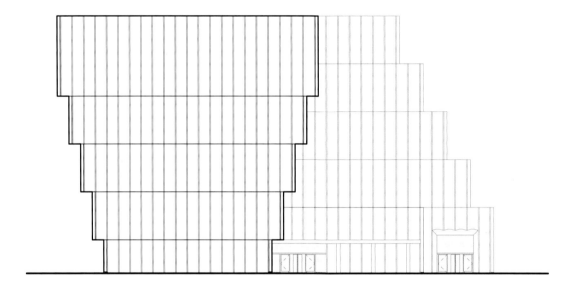

EAST ELEVATION

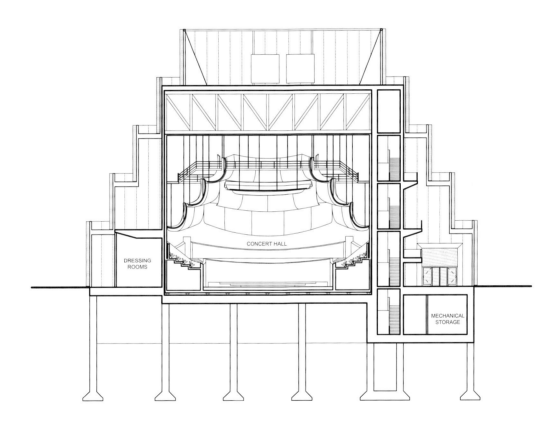

DRESSING
ROOMS

CONCERT HALL

MECHANICAL
STORAGE

SECTION B

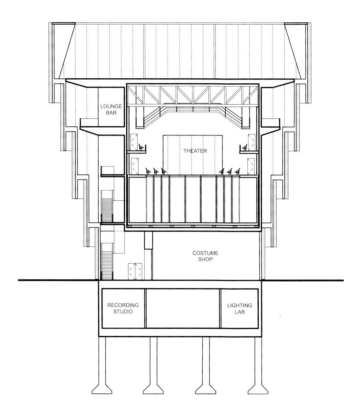

LOUNGE BAR

THEATER

COSTUME SHOP

RECORDING STUDIO

LIGHTING LAB

SECTION C

The inverted pyramid form of the theater volume to the east stretches upwards towards the Chicago skyline, over Halsted Avenue and the expressways, putting the theater at the crux of city and campus, while maintaining a small footprint at the street level. The theater box is lifted within the stepped glass form, creating a procession from the plateau via a sculptural stair into the hall. Panoramic views of the campus and the city are revealed from the surrounding lobbies on the third and fourth floors. The theater space is envisioned to be an extension of the urban campus landscape—an informal assemblage of infrastructure systems with flexibility to accommodate various stage and seating arrangements. In dramatic fashion, the scene dock can be opened to expand the performance area to the east with a large glass window affording a view to downtown Chicago.

Concert hall

Theater

RICE UNIVERSITY VISUAL & DRAMATIC ARTS

HOUSTON, TEXAS (2020)

Rice University Visual & Dramatic Arts Building, with Moody Center beyond

VADA Phase I

The design for VADA is a mountainous landscape defining the campus edge and dedicated to creative production; with a distinct expression on each elevation, it draws on different eras of material history at Rice, creating specific relationships to campus buildings and landscape. The western entrance is articulated by a large canopy that provides shaded informal space on a raised front porch framed by undulating woven brickwork to distinguish the entry. The surrounding green connects VADA and the Moody Center as an informal social space marked by the historic tree planted by Andy Warhol. To the north, the metal-clad roof wraps down the facade, framing the neighboring Moody with a material similar in tone. A pedestrian street connects the two arts facilities as it demarcates a new outdoor space for engagement, mirroring the informal streets within VADA. The eastern facade articulates the kit-of-parts nature of the design and the potential for future expansion in each project phase. At the south, the facade marks the campus edge with traditional, variegated brickwork, linking the identity of the building to the architectural legacy of Rice. Reflecting the interdisciplinary nature of VADA, the facades coalesce into a building that represents the diverse identity of the program imbued with the spirit of the campus history.

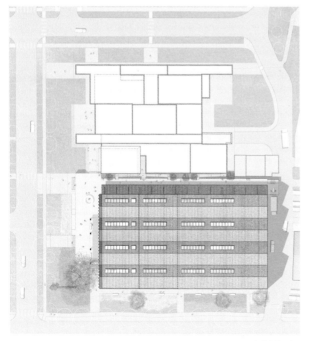

Aerial site plan

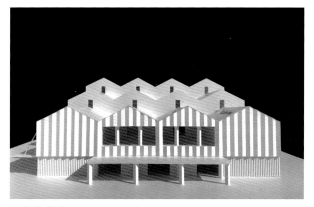
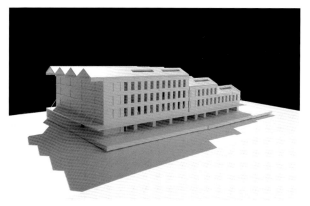
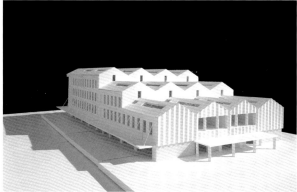
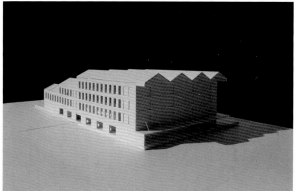

VADA Phase II model photos

Open classroom and studio space

By combining elements of the factory building and the palazzo, VADA brings together vast, functional space for making, alongside rooms for determined and focused engagement to support the full exploratory arc of interdisciplinary study. Public spaces for viewing art are balanced with inward-oriented spaces for student experimentation and production. Voluminous, adaptable spaces are linked to disciplinary-specific spaces through generous interstitial circulation areas. Connectivity and reciprocity unfold across the interior through 'streets' connecting flexible physical spaces and accommodating reciprocal uses and temporal exchange. Designed as a kit-of-parts, the building provides an expansive, future-oriented environment that can adapt to changing art practices.

Envisioned as a workplace dedicated to students, the design provides a range of spaces that foster interdisciplinary study and support a creative ecology throughout—a building of today, with flexibility and longevity to evolve alongside the VADA program.

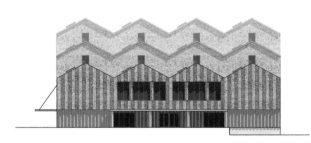

Elevations of four distinct facades: (from top to bottom) east, west, north and south

Central stair connecting VADA programs

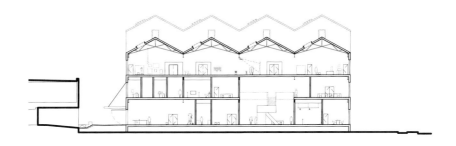

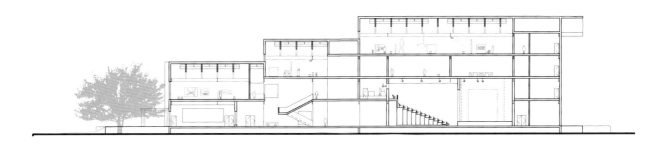

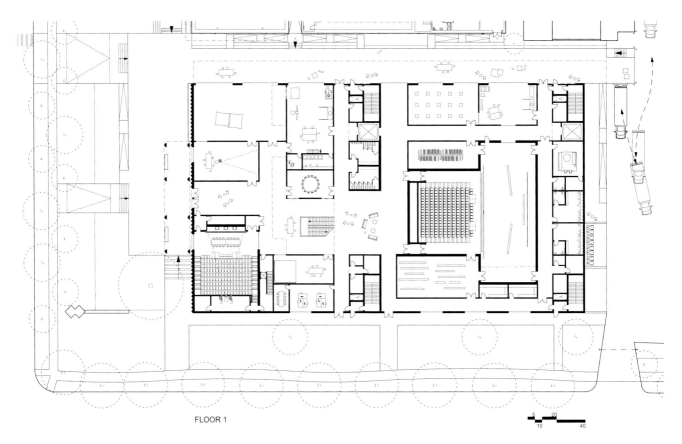

FLOOR 1

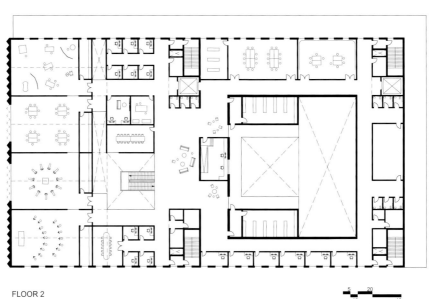

FLOOR 2

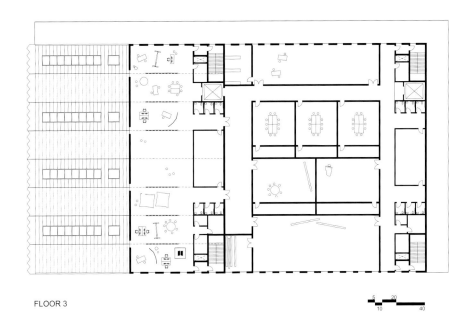

FLOOR 3

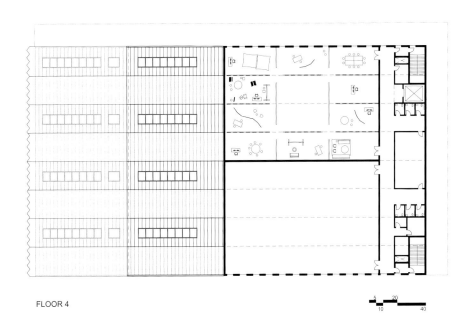

FLOOR 4

MCA CHICAGO

CHICAGO, ILLINOIS (2017)

Aerial site image

Northeast corner and re-envisioned plinth

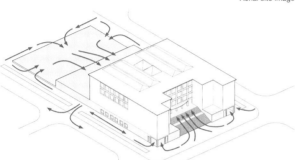

Circulation diagram

East elevation: proposed terrace and sculpture garden

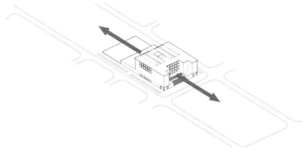

Circulation diagram

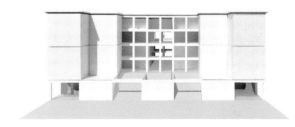

West elevation

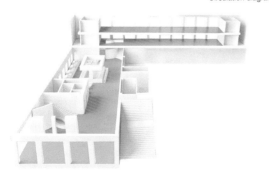

Model of Phase I renovation

The master plan for the Museum of Contemporary Art Chicago (MCA) aligns the museum with the legacy of Chicago: a city of museums situated in magnificent parks. The analysis of the MCA—which was designed by Josef Paul Kleihues and completed in 1996—considered the identity of the museum at multiple scales: from the perspective of the city, the precinct of Michigan Avenue to the lake, and the immediate block surrounded by parks to the east and west. Coupled with this urban vision, the work was guided by the MCA's mission to be an artist-activated and audience-engaged institution.

The first phase of the renovation plan strengthens the museum's connection to the city at street level while elevating the sanctity of the museum above. The plans integrate signature elements of the Kleihues building—including the regulating grid, the shipshape stair, and the vaulted ceiling—while introducing new spaces for contemporary artists and audiences to meet. With a focus on enhanced public space, the renovation reframes the museum experience as a more flexible, generous, light-filled environment.

New entry and theater lounge

New public stair connecting ground floor to museum level

Engagement zone as flexible space

Framed by a crypt-like vaulted ceiling that recalls the vaults of the fourth floor galleries above, a new interior street at the ground level unites museum visitors with theater patrons in and around the relocated restaurant and bar, eroding the rigidity of the Kleihues grid. A stair at the end of this street affords natural light from the east into the base of the building, forming a continuous public space linking the lower level to the new commons space on the second floor and the east sculpture terrace. A new floor within the double-height volume of the commons is integrated into the strict structural grid system of the building; it provides classroom and meeting space in the heart of the museum with views of the lake and the four-story entry atrium.

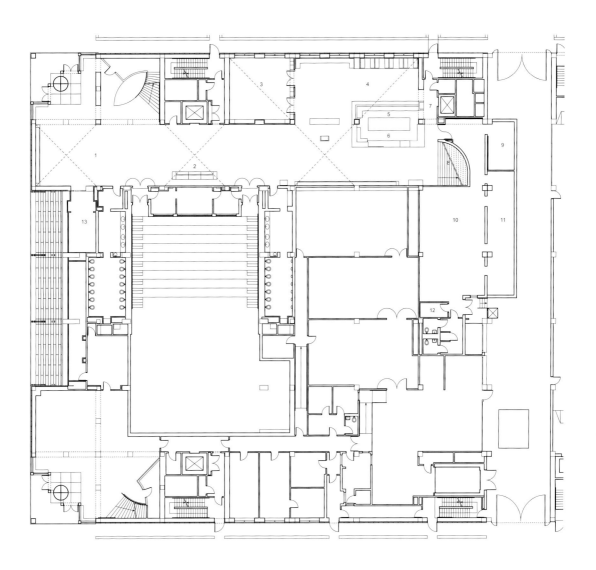

FIRST FLOOR

1. LOBBY
2. TICKET COUNTER
3. PRIVATE DINING
4. RESTAURANT
5. BAR
6. TAKE AWAY
7. CORRIDOR
8. CONVENIENCE STAIR
9. DISHWASHING
10. KITCHEN
11. KITCHEN ANNEX
12. CHEF'S OFFICE
13. COATROOM

FT
0 1 5   10   40

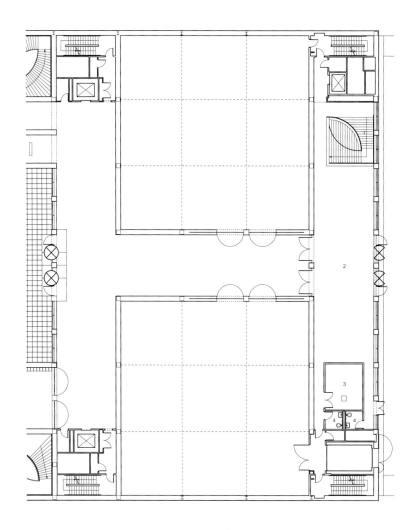

SECOND FLOOR

1. CONVENIENCE STAIR
2. COMMONS
3. PANTRY
4. W/C

FT
0 1 5   10   40

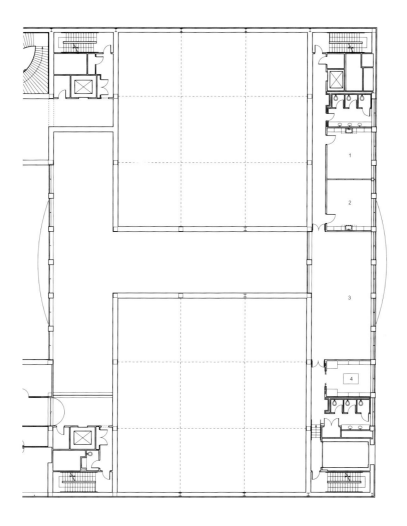

THIRD FLOOR

1. EDUCATION STUDIO 1
2. EDUCATION STUDIO 2
3. MULTIPURPOSE ROOM
4. WORKROOM

FT
0 1 5   10   40

CASA DE MONT

PACIFIC PALISADES, CALIFORNIA (2019)

Casa de Mont is located on a prominent ridge along a canyon in Pacific Palisades, California. The parcel is oriented towards the south, with open views towards the ocean to the southwest. The sweeping profile of the house is achieved from splitting one mass into two curved volumes in response to the topography of the canyon and the street.

Reflecting the double massing, the house is a hybrid of two types of villas. Towards the north, the carved stone facade is modulated by a gridded framework which recalls the language of pilaster and entablature, marking the underlying structure of the house and projecting a formal language towards the street. On the south elevation, with views to the ocean, the underlying grid is embedded into the stucco envelope and marked only by the consistent rhythm of window openings and the columns of the extended roof. Defined by the sweeping porch across the length of the facade, the Mediterranean tradition of shaded porches, deep windows, and crisp shadows engages the house with the legacy of living inside and out in Southern California.

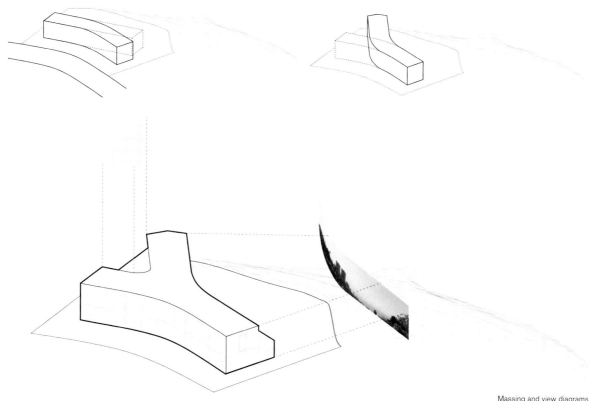

Massing and view diagrams

The distribution of program reflects the split in the mass, with the secondary programs including the garage, guest rooms, entry, den, and gym oriented towards the street. The primary programs of the kitchen, dining room, living room, office, and the master suite on the second floor are oriented towards the south. Along the southern facade, a continuous porch forms an in-between space connecting inside and outside living areas. As a shaded patio, the canopy softens the southern light from the interior of the house, providing the ideal controlled light environment for art. An art gallery is tucked between the two volumes; the triangular plan is oriented around a central skylight which brings diffused northern light into the gallery.

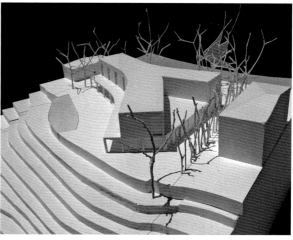

Above and next page: Model photos of Casa de Mont

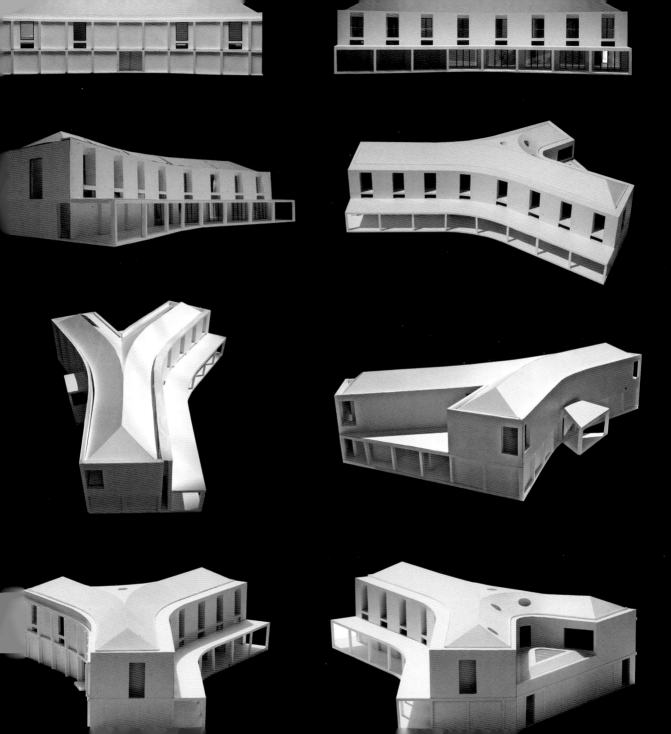

North elevation

South elevation

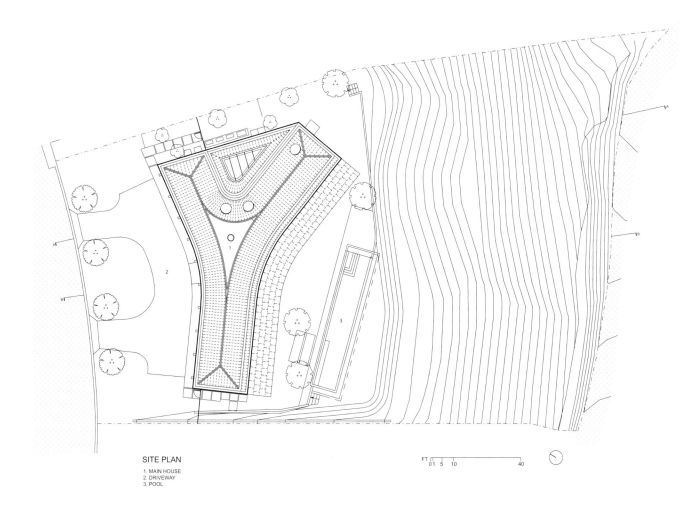

SITE PLAN

1. MAIN HOUSE
2. DRIVEWAY
3. POOL

FT
0 1 5 10   40

The house is organized as a sequence of rooms, separated
by poché walls, that inscribe the structural bay into the depth
of the plan, and are dedicated to the client's art collection.
Fluid circulation—allowing different flows between rooms—
characterizes the floor plan, where all spaces are primary environments for art and view. Variations in atmosphere, scale,
and material cladding mark the transitions in use. A double
height entry mixes light from a north-facing vertical window
with a south-facing skylight while orienting circulation on the
ground floor and connecting to the second level from a new
stair. Upstairs, a low light, continuous-circulation gallery for
drawings and works on paper connects the sleeping rooms.

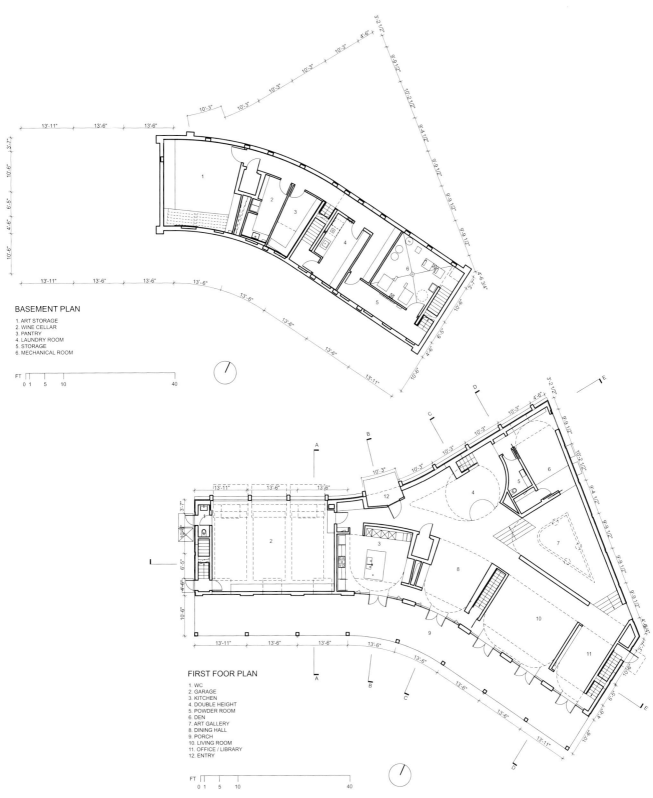

BASEMENT PLAN

1. ART STORAGE
2. WINE CELLAR
3. PANTRY
4. LAUNDRY ROOM
5. STORAGE
6. MECHANICAL ROOM

FT
0 1   5   10   40

FIRST FOOR PLAN

1. WC
2. GARAGE
3. KITCHEN
4. DOUBLE HEIGHT
5. POWDER ROOM
6. DEN
7. ART GALLERY
8. DINING HALL
9. PORCH
10. LIVING ROOM
11. OFFICE / LIBRARY
12. ENTRY

FT
0 1   5   10   40

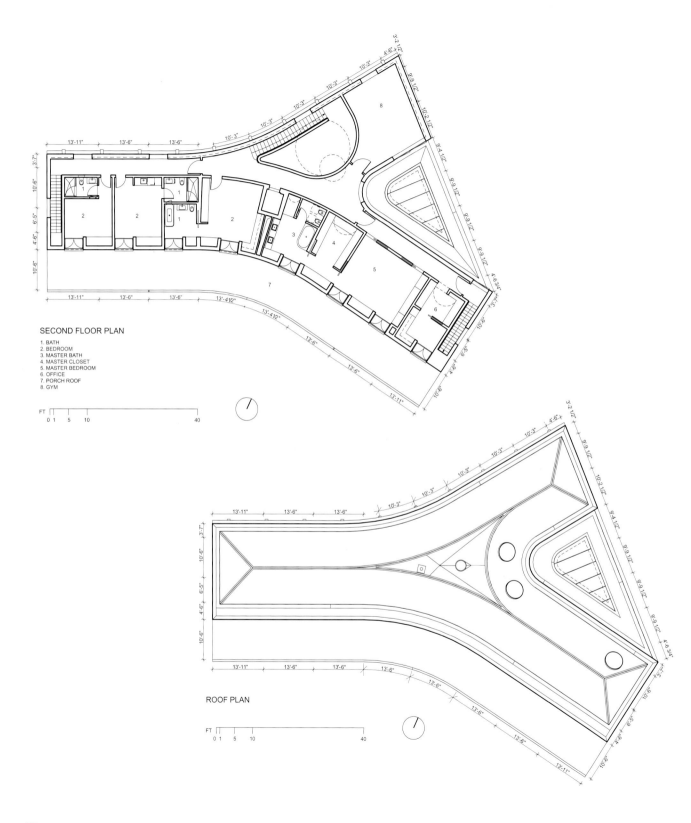

SECOND FLOOR PLAN

1. BATH
2. BEDROOM
3. MASTER BATH
4. MASTER CLOSET
5. MASTER BEDROOM
6. OFFICE
7. PORCH ROOF
8. GYM

FT
0 1   5   10   40

ROOF PLAN

FT
0 1   5   10   40

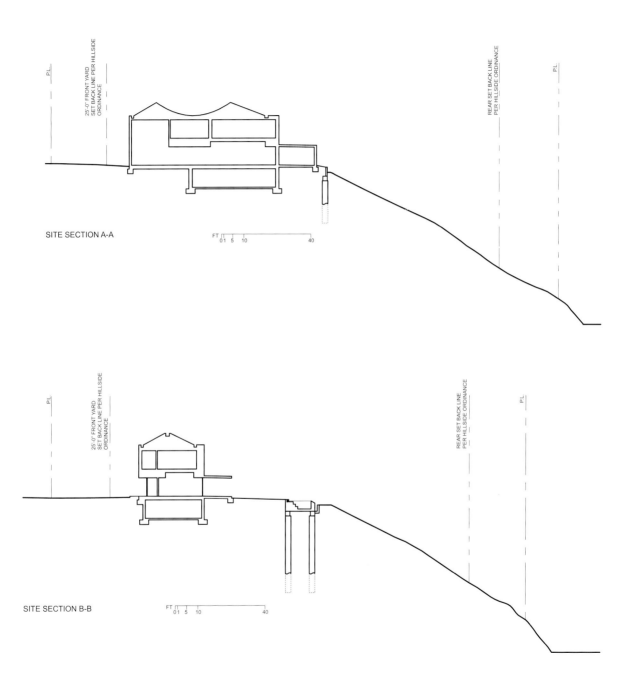

PL

25'-0" FRONT YARD
SET BACK LINE PER HILLSIDE
ORDINANCE

REAR SET BACK LINE
PER HILLSIDE ORDINANCE

PL

SITE SECTION A-A

FT
0 1 5   10   40

PL

25'-0" FRONT YARD
SET BACK LINE PER HILLSIDE
ORDINANCE

REAR SET BACK LINE
PER HILLSIDE ORDINANCE

PL

SITE SECTION B-B

FT
0 1 5   10   40

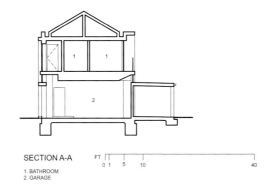

SECTION A-A   FT
                0 1 5   10   40

1. BATHROOM
2. GARAGE

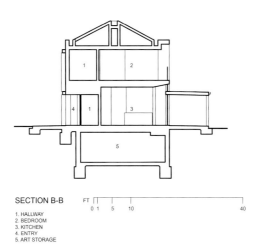

SECTION B-B   FT
                0 1 5   10   40

1. HALLWAY
2. BEDROOM
3. KITCHEN
4. ENTRY
5. ART STORAGE

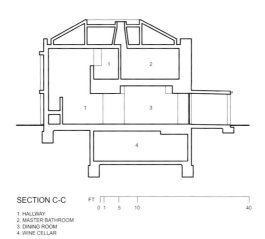

SECTION C-C   FT
                0 1 5   10   40

1. HALLWAY
2. MASTER BATHROOM
3. DINING ROOM
4. WINE CELLAR

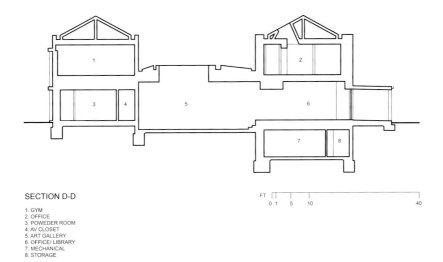

SECTION D-D

1. GYM
2. OFFICE
3. POWEDER ROOM
4. AV CLOSET
5. ART GALLERY
6. OFFICE/ LIBRARY
7. MECHANICAL
8. STORAGE

FT
0 1   5   10   40

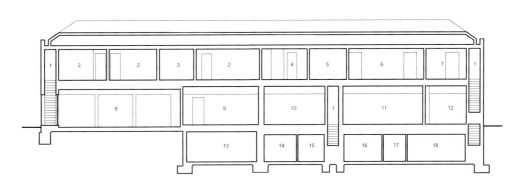

SECTION E-E

1. STAIR
2. BEDROOM
3. BATHROOM
4. MASTER BATHROOM
5. MASTER CLOSET
6. MASTER BEDROOM
7. OFFICE
8. GARAGE
9. KITCHEN
10. DINING
11. LIVING ROOM
12. OFFICE/ LIBRARY
13. ART STORAGE
14. WINE CELLAR
15. PANTRY
16. LAUNDRY ROOM
17. HALLWAY
18. MECHANICAL ROOM

FT
0 1   5   10   40

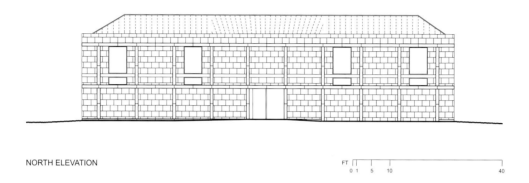

NORTH ELEVATION

FT ⌐‾
0 1   5   10   40

SOUTH ELEVATION

FT ⌐‾
0 1   5   10   40

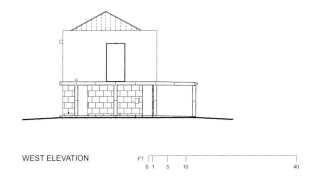

WEST ELEVATION

FT
0 1 5 10   40

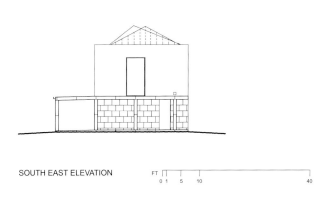

SOUTH EAST ELEVATION

FT
0 1 5 10   40

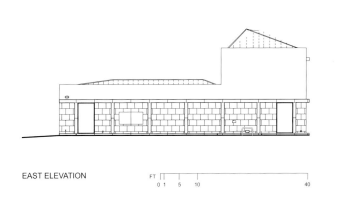

EAST ELEVATION

FT
0 1 5 10   40

PORCH HOUSE

LOS ANGELES, CALIFORNIA (2013)

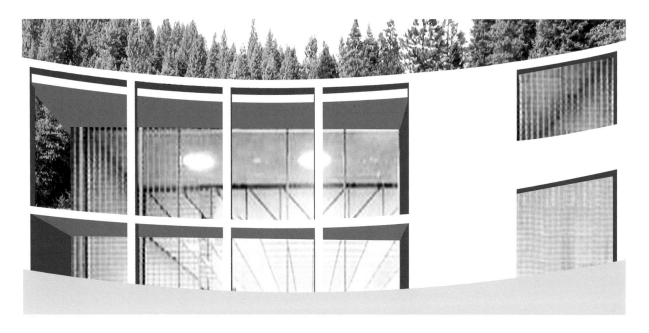

The Porch House sits on a plateau at the top of a steeply-sloping meadow, facing a state park and the ocean beyond. The existing hillside is untouched, stabilized by a curved retaining wall that allows the house to be built very close to the edge of the site. The curve of the southwest facade of the building bends to match the existing terrain, underscoring the natural contour of the landscape.

The massing is made up of two volumes. The first, a solid, encloses the garage and the split-level mezzanine, mediating the topological difference between the street and the site. This volume is most visible from the street. The second mass, an open frame, encloses spaces for living and for entertaining, defined by a structural concrete colonnade. The space between the colonnade and the glass box—between the curve of the landscape and the volume of the house—echoes the typology of the historical American porch, which has long negotiated between the private interior and the world outside. Here, the whole house becomes porch.

While the standard house typology typically provides living space on the ground floor and locates private rooms above, the Porch House is reversed to maintain an unbroken progression from the street. Entering the house directly on the second floor, the main living space floors are finished in terrazzo and concrete. This configuration allows the living room to expand vertically; the material order similarly extends horizontally to the porch. Bedrooms below conform to the logic of the tetrastyle colonnade above but are rendered materially in wood.

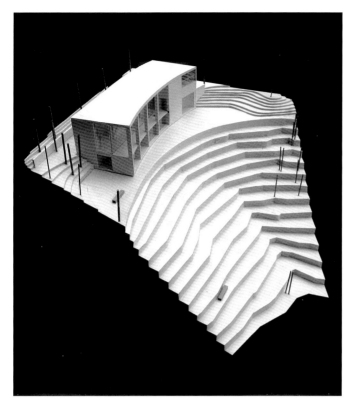

Site model

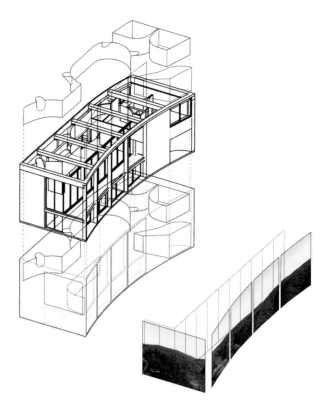

Axonometric and view diagram

West elevation

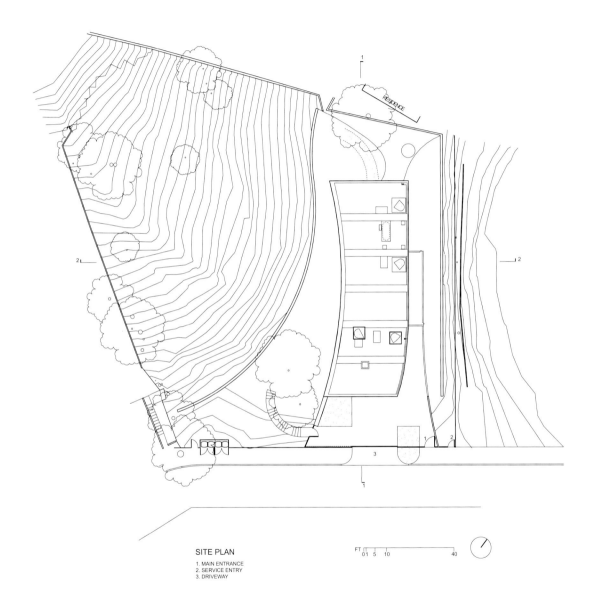

SITE PLAN

1. MAIN ENTRANCE
2. SERVICE ENTRY
3. DRIVEWAY

FT 01 5 10   40

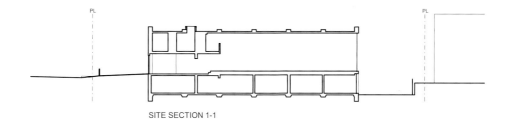

SITE SECTION 1-1

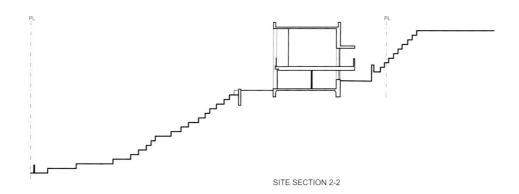

SITE SECTION 2-2

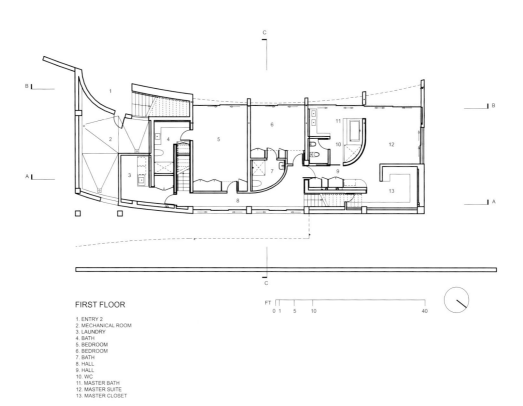

FIRST FLOOR

1. ENTRY 2
2. MECHANICAL ROOM
3. LAUNDRY
4. BATH
5. BEDROOM
6. BEDROOM
7. BATH
8. HALL
9. HALL
10. WC
11. MASTER BATH
12. MASTER SUITE
13. MASTER CLOSET

FT
0 1   5   10   40

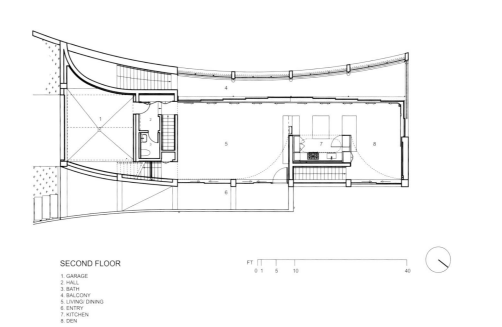

SECOND FLOOR

1. GARAGE
2. HALL
3. BATH
4. BALCONY
5. LIVING/ DINING
6. ENTRY
7. KITCHEN
8. DEN

FT
0 1   5   10   40

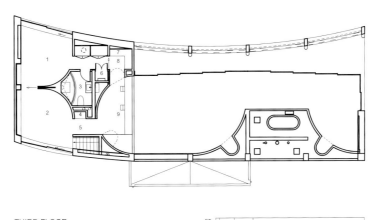

THIRD FLOOR

1. EXERCISE ROOM
2. LOUNGE
3. BATH
4. BOOKSHELF
5. LIBRARY
6. ROOF ACCESS
7. BOOKSHELF
8. LIBRARY
9. OFFICE

FT
0 1   5   10   40

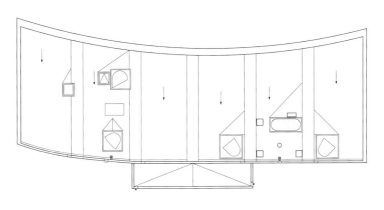

ROOF PLAN

FT
0 1   5   10   40

Living room

Northwest corner

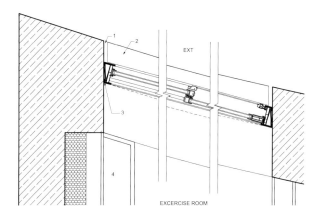

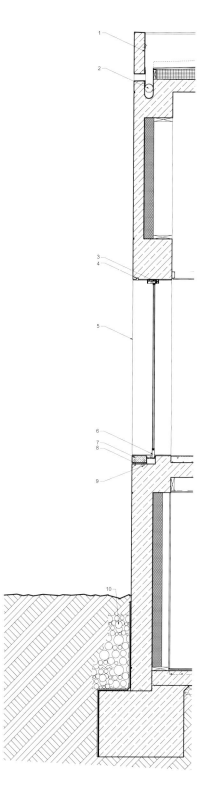

DETAIL - PLAN WINDOW

1. 1" GAP
2. PRECAST CONCRETE SILL
3. ALUMINUM ANGLE
4. BOOKSHELF

EXT

EXCERCISE ROOM

DETAIL - FIXED WINDOW

1. TPO FLASHING DETAIL TBD
2. INTEGRATED 5' PIPE GUTTER THROUGH
   STRUCTURAL INVERTED BEAM BEYOND
3. SURFACE MOUNTED WINDOW SYSTEM
4. DRIP EDGE
5. COLUMN BEYOND PER STRUCTURAL
6. SURFACE MOUNTED WINDOW SYSTEM
7. CONCRETE SILL
8. 1/2" DRIP GAB
9. ANCHORS PER STRUCTURAL
10. VEGETATED SWALE PER CIVIL

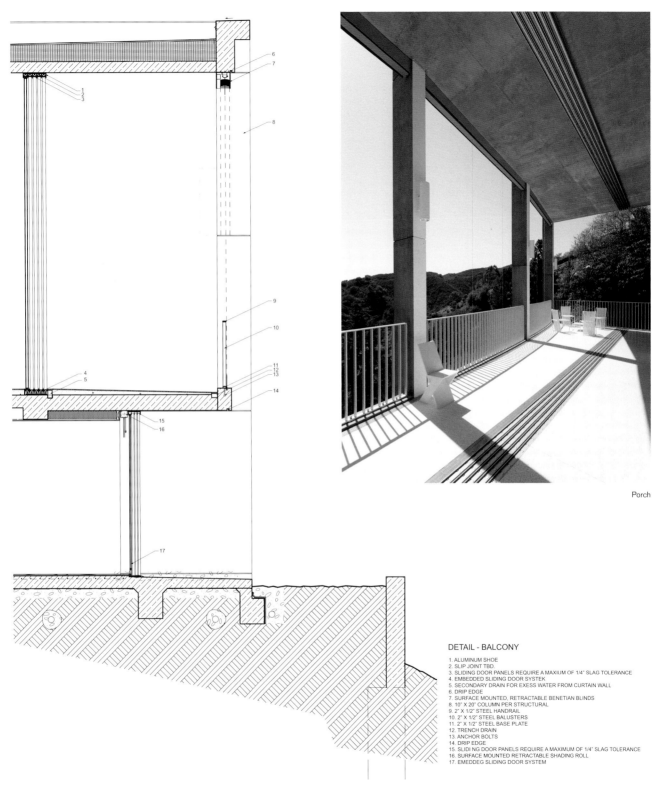

Porch

DETAIL - BALCONY

1. ALUMINUM SHOE
2. SLIP JOINT TBD.
3. SLIDING DOOR PANELS REQUIRE A MAXIUM OF 1/4" SLAG TOLERANCE
4. EMBEDDED SLIDING DOOR SYSTEK
5. SECONDARY DRAIN FOR EXESS WATER FROM CURTAIN WALL
6. DRIP EDGE
7. SURFACE MOUNTED, RETRACTABLE BENETIAN BLINDS
8. 10" X 20" COLUMN PER STRUCTURAL
9. 2" X 1/2" STEEL HANDRAIL
10. 2" X 1/2" STEEL BALUSTERS
11. 2" X 1/2" STEEL BASE PLATE
12. TRENCH DRAIN
13. ANCHOR BOLTS
14. DRIP EDGE
15. SLIDI NG DOOR PANELS REQUIRE A MAXIMUM OF 1/4" SLAG TOLERANCE
16. SURFACE MOUNTED RETRACTABLE SHADING ROLL
17. EMEDDEG SLIDING DOOR SYSTEM

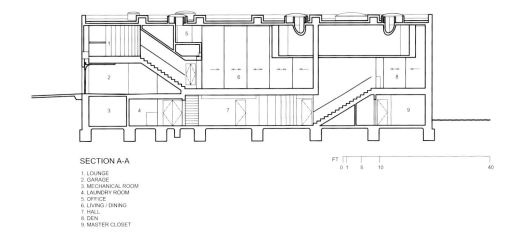

SECTION A-A

1. LOUNGE
2. GARAGE
3. MECHANICAL ROOM
4. LAUNDRY ROOM
5. OFFICE
6. LIVING / DINING
7. HALL
8. DEN
9. MASTER CLOSET

FT
0 1   5   10   40

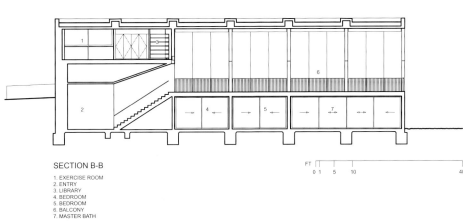

SECTION B-B

1. EXERCISE ROOM
2. ENTRY
3. LIBRARY
4. BEDROOM
5. BEDROOM
6. BALCONY
7. MASTER BATH

FT
0 1   5   10   40

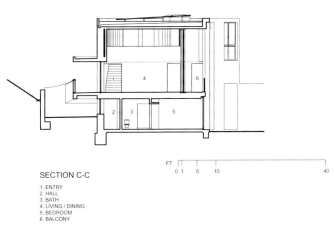

SECTION C-C

1. ENTRY
2. HALL
3. BATH
4. LIVING / DINING
5. BEDROOM
6. BALCONY

FT
0 1   5   10   40

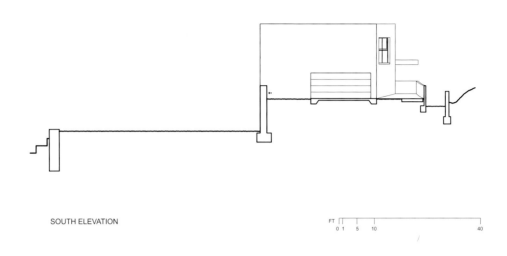

SOUTH ELEVATION

FT
0 1   5   10   40

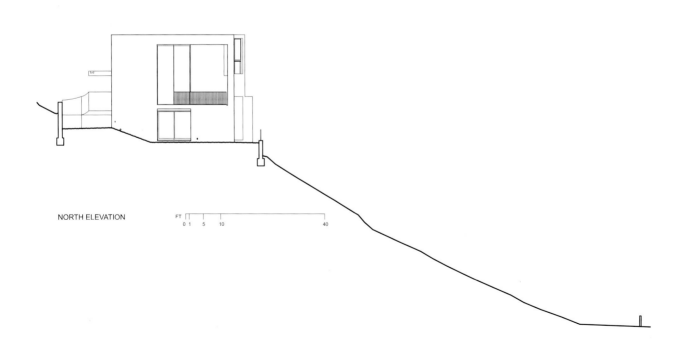

NORTH ELEVATION

FT
0 1   5   10   40

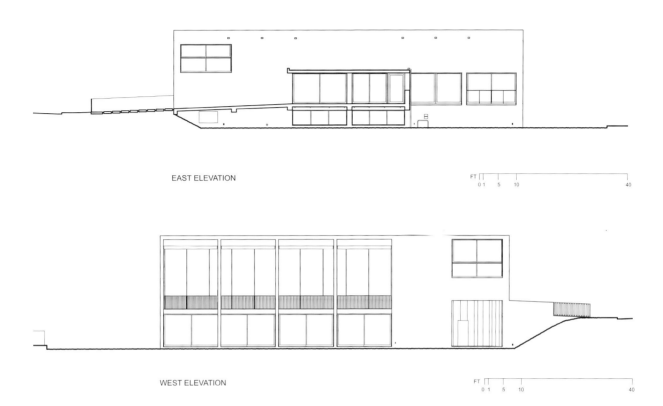

EAST ELEVATION

FT 0 1 5 10 40

WEST ELEVATION

FT 0 1 5 10 40

West elevation

HUT HOUSE

KAUAI, HAWAII (2014)

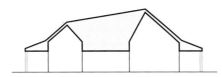

Sectional compression and expansion

Hut House is a hybrid of the traditional Hawaiian roof typology and a Spanish court-yard typology with a central courtyard as a private retreat from the perimeter veranda or 'lanai.' The extreme climate demanded programmatic distribution of the house into a micro village, with four distinct volumes arranged around the courtyard protected under a single roof. By placing the volumes casually under the monolithic roof, the lanai is broken into a series of distinct places oriented toward specific views of the panoramic landscape.

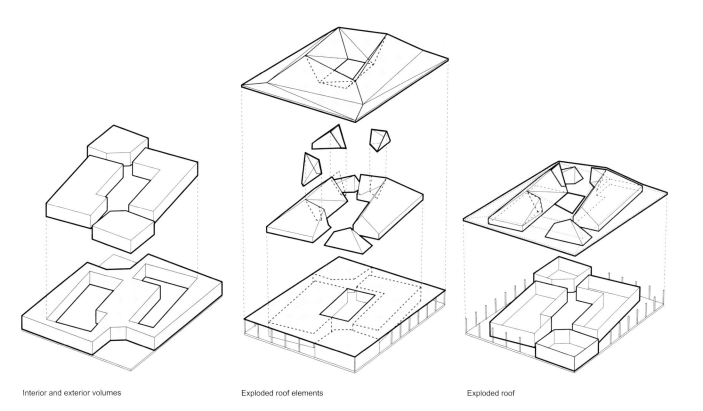

Interior and exterior volumes

Exploded roof elements

Exploded roof

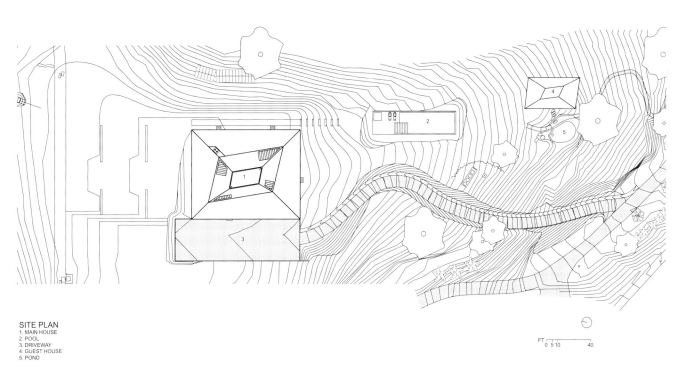

SITE PLAN
1. MAIN HOUSE
2. POOL
3. DRIVEWAY
4. GUEST HOUSE
5. POND

FT
0 5 10   40

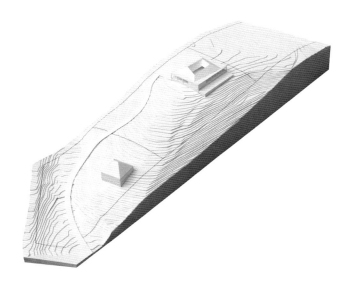
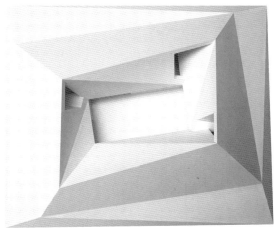

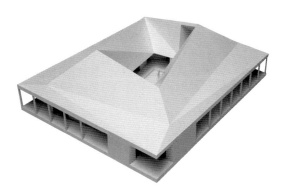
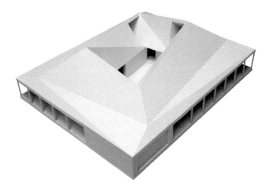

Site and aerial model views

Skylight detail form above

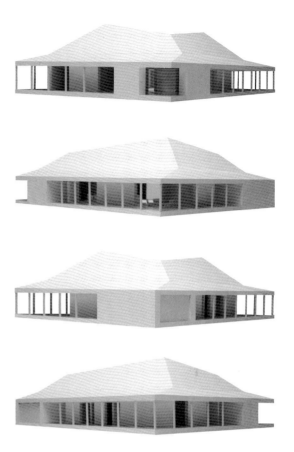

Model elevations

Courtyard details

Hut House

Hut House

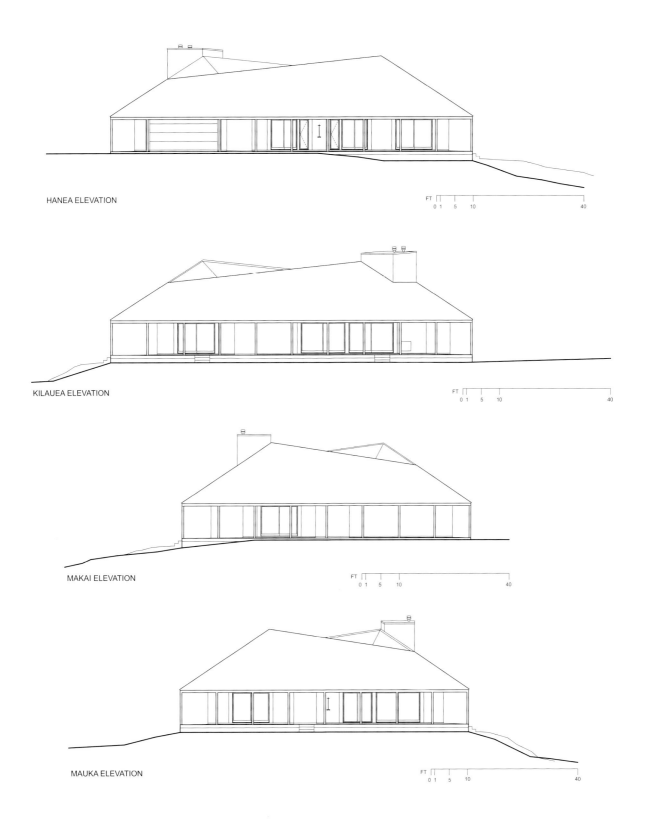

HANEA ELEVATION

FT
0 1 5 10   40

KILAUEA ELEVATION

FT
0 1 5 10   40

MAKAI ELEVATION

FT
0 1 5 10   40

MAUKA ELEVATION

FT
0 1 5 10   40

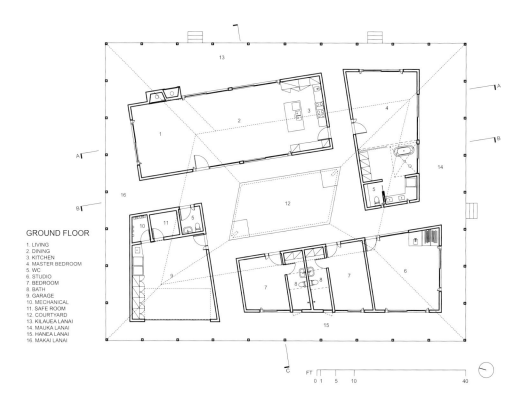

GROUND FLOOR

1. LIVING
2. DINING
3. KITCHEN
4. MASTER BEDROOM
5. WC
6. STUDIO
7. BEDROOM
8. BATH
9. GARAGE
10. MECHANICAL
11. SAFE ROOM
12. COURTYARD
13. KILAUEA LANAI
14. MAUKA LANAI
15. HANEA LANAI
16. MAKAI LANAI

FT
0 1   5   10   40

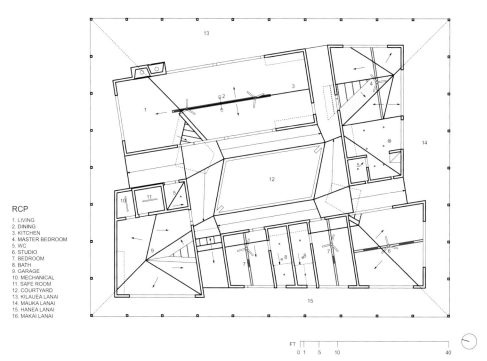

RCP

1. LIVING
2. DINING
3. KITCHEN
4. MASTER BEDROOM
5. WC
6. STUDIO
7. BEDROOM
8. BATH
9. GARAGE
10. MECHANICAL
11. SAFE ROOM
12. COURTYARD
13. KILAUEA LANAI
14. MAUKA LANAI
15. HANEA LANAI
16. MAKAI LANAI

FT
0 1   5   10   40

Courtyard

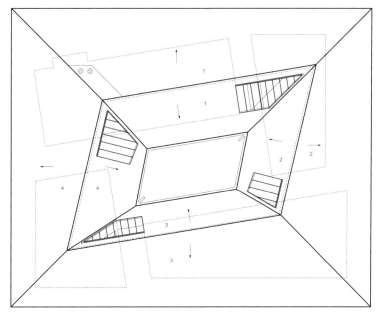

ROOF

1. KILAUEA LANAI
2. MAUKA LANAI
3. HANEA LANAI
4. MAKAI LANAI

FT
0 1   5   10   40

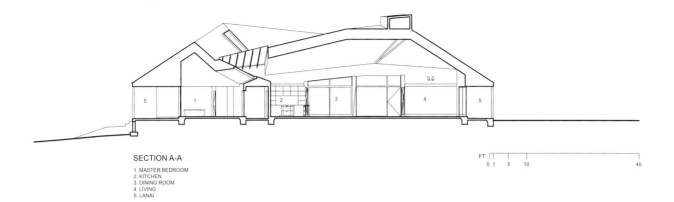

SECTION A-A

1. MASTER BEDROOM
2. KITCHEN
3. DINING ROOM
4. LIVING
5. LANAI

FT
0 1   5   10   40

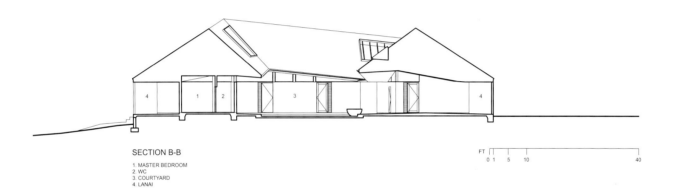

SECTION B-B

1. MASTER BEDROOM
2. WC
3. COURTYARD
4. LANAI

FT
0 1   5   10   40

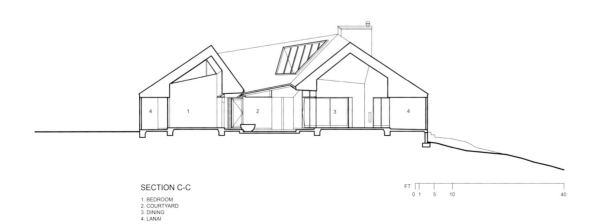

SECTION C-C

1. BEDROOM
2. COURTYARD
3. DINING
4. LANAI

FT
0 1   5   10   40

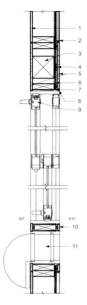

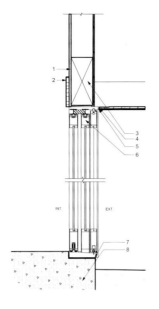

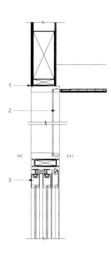

DETAIL - WINDOW PLAN

1. GYPSUM BOARD
2. VINYL CASSING BEAD, TYP.
3. POST PER STRL. WHERE OCCURS
4. FURRING AS NEEDED
5. SOLID WOOD TRIM
6. WEATHER BARRIER
7. TAPE FLASHING AT ROUGH OPENINGS, TYP.
8. JOINT SEALANT
9. LIFT AND SLIDE UNITS
10. SOLID WOOD TRIM
11. VENTILATION UNIT

DETAIL - WINDOW SECTION

1. GYPSUM BOARD
2. WOOD TRIM BAORD
3. HEADER PER STRL.
4. VINYL CASSING BEAD, TYP.
5. JOINT SEALANT
6. LIFT AND SLIDE UNIT
7. SILL PAN
8. CONCRETE SLAB PER STRL.

DETAIL - SECTION W/ CLERSTORY ABOVE

1. MUDABLE J BEAD TYP. VINYL
2. FIXED WINDOW
3. LIFT AND SLIDE UNIT

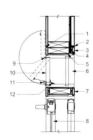

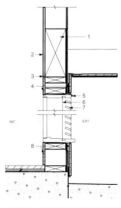

DETAIL - VENTILATION UNIT PLAN

1. MUDDABLE J BEAD TYP. VINYL
2. JOINT SEALANT TYP.
3. SOLID WOOD TRIM
4. FURRING AS NEEDED
5. WEATHER BARRIER
6. FIXED LOUVERS
7. SOLID WOOD TRIM
8. SLIDING GLASS DOOR
9. FULL MORTISE HINGE, BRUSHED CHROME
10. DOOR PANEL
11. CASEMENT FASTNER DELTANA CF066 US32D
12. CABIN SWIVEL HOOK DELTANA CHK4 US32D

DETAIL - VENTILATION UNIT SECTION

1. HEADER PER STRL.
2. GYPSUM BOARD
3. MUDDABLE J BEAD TYP. VINYL
4. SOLID WOOD TRIM
5. DRIP CAP
6. SCREEN
7. FIXED LOUVERS
8. SOLID WOOD TRIM

Entry lanai

Living and dining room

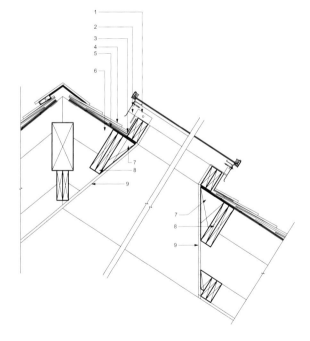

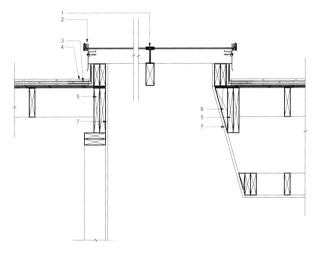

DETAIL - SKYLIGHT VERTICAL SECTION

1. CUSTOM FIXED FLAT GLASS SKYLIGHT
2. VENTING THROUGH SKYLIGHT
3. FLASHING
4. WOOD SHAKES
5. SHEATHING PER STRL.
6. 2X RAFTER PER STRL.
7. SOLID BLOCKING
8. RAFTER PER STRL.
9. GYPSUM WALL BOARD

DETAIL - SKYLIGHT HORIZONTAL SECTION

1. MULLION
2. CUSTOM FIXED FLAT SKYLIGHT UNIT
3. STEPPED FLASHING
4. WOOD SHINGLES
5. RAFTERS PER STRL.
6. SOLID BLOCKING
7. GYPSUM WALL BAORD

PHILADELPHIA CONTEMPORARY

PHILADELPHIA, PENNSYLVANIA (2019)

South plaza

Southeast corner

Southwest elevation

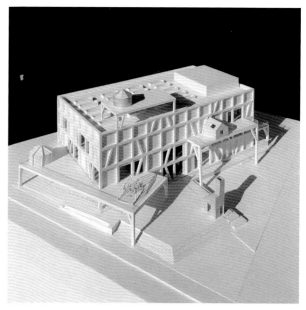

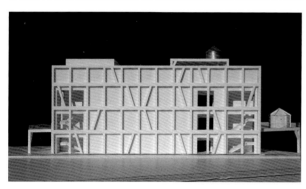

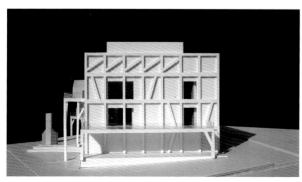

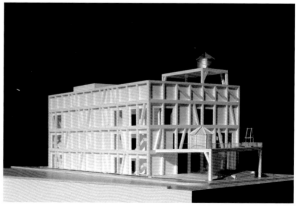

Model views

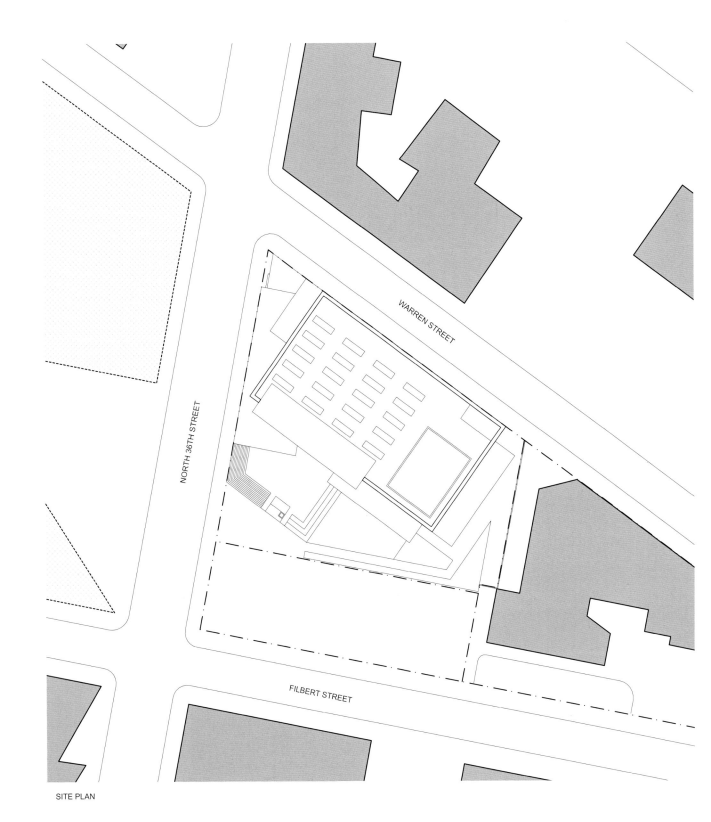

WARREN STREET

NORTH 36TH STREET

FILBERT STREET

SITE PLAN

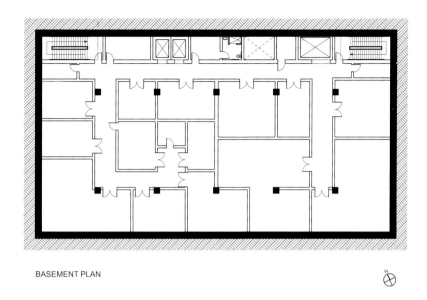

BASEMENT PLAN

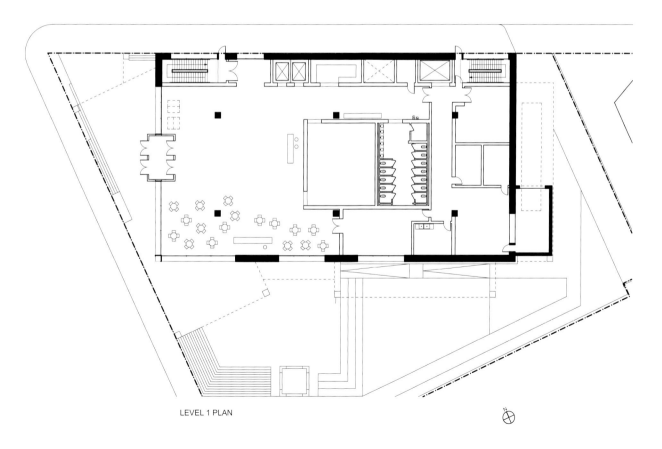

LEVEL 1 PLAN

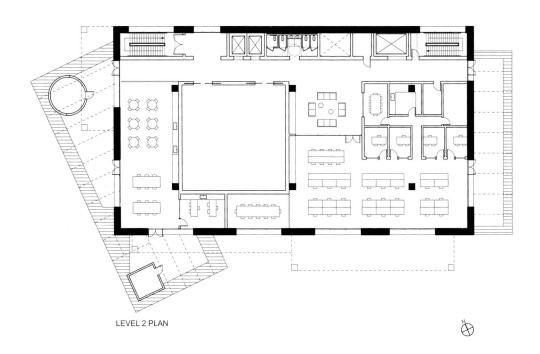

LEVEL 2 PLAN

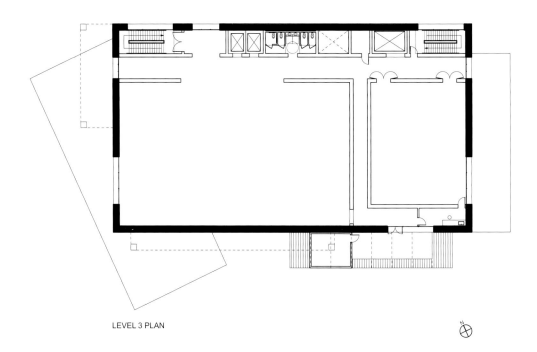

LEVEL 3 PLAN

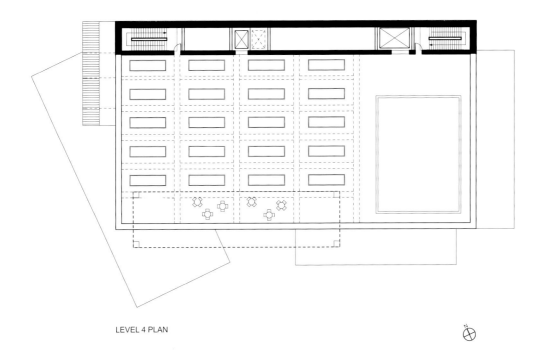

LEVEL 4 PLAN

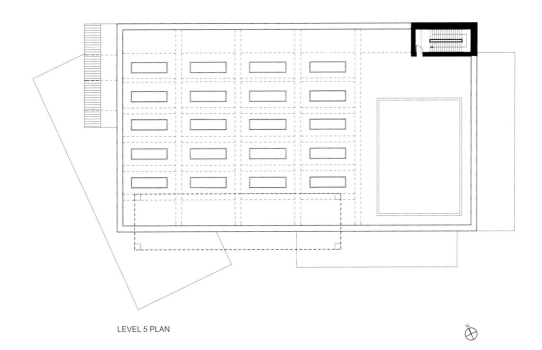

LEVEL 5 PLAN

SOUTH ELEVATION

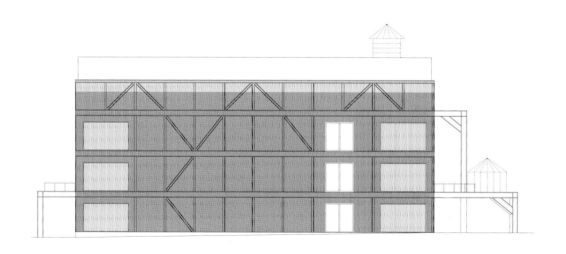

SOUTH ELEVATION

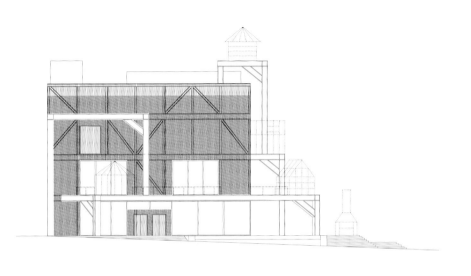

WEST ELEVATION

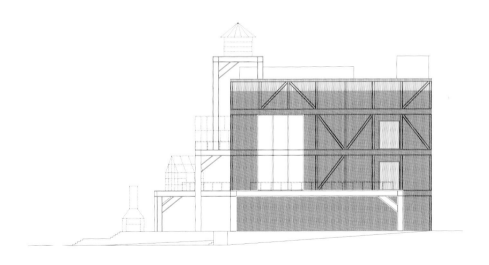

EAST ELEVATION

MIAMI DESIGN DISTRICT

MIAMI, FLORIDA (2017)

The Miami Design District is a new commercial development in the once-industrial neighborhood of Buena Vista, Miami. Planning principles from the master plan developed by DPZ founders Andres Duany and Elizabeth Plater-Zyberk include walkable streets and passageways, shade gardens, and rooftop landscapes, formed by a collection of discrete architectural projects and art installations in a diverse but coherent fabric. Johnston Marklee's facade arcade frames the north end of Paradise Plaza, which terminates the new central walk street of Paseo Ponti. The paseo spans the extent of the four-block development and the new plaza includes a garden with a site specific art installation. The JML facade is defined by a structural frame which forms the curtain wall at the ground level, defines the open-air arcade on the second level, and extends as a parapet to frame the rooftop garden and the sky beyond, visible from the length of the four-block paseo. The rationalist grid is wrapped in a concave, curved, stainless steel cladding system of reflective and abraded panels. Stripped of ornament, the curved surfaces are modeled and amplified by natural light. The consistency of detail from the plaza scale to the city scale reflects the presence of the building as part of the larger urban fabric.

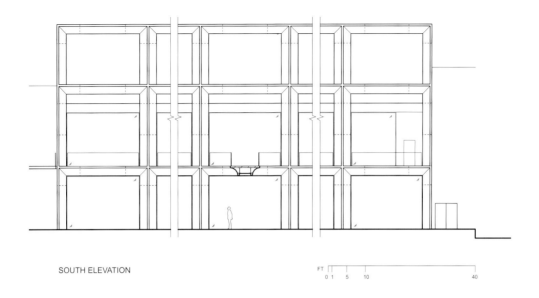

SOUTH ELEVATION

FT
0 1   5   10   40

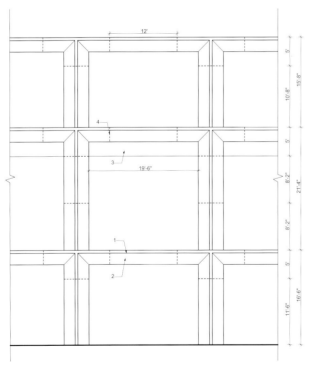

12'

5'
15'-8"
10'-8"

4

3

19'-6"

5'
8'-2"
21'-4"

1

8'-2"

2

5'

11'-6"
16'-6"

SOUTH ELEVATION

1. POLISHED STAINLESS STEEL TRIM
2. CURVED BRUSHED STAINLESS PANEL
3. FLAT BRUSHED STAINLESS PANEL
4. SEAM LINES BETWEEN PREFABRICATED PANELS

Facade detail

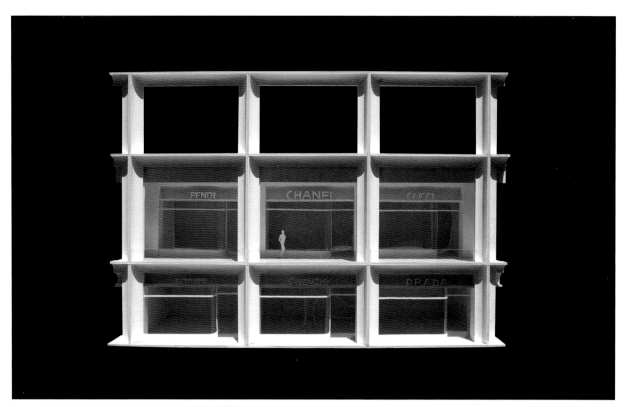

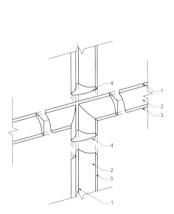

AXONOMETRIC CONNECTION

1. POLISHED STAINLESS STEEL TRIM
2. CURVED BRUSHED STAINLESS PANEL
3. FLAT BRUSHED STAINLESS PANEL
4. SEAM LINES BETWEEN PREFABRICATED PANELS

Model images

Facade detail

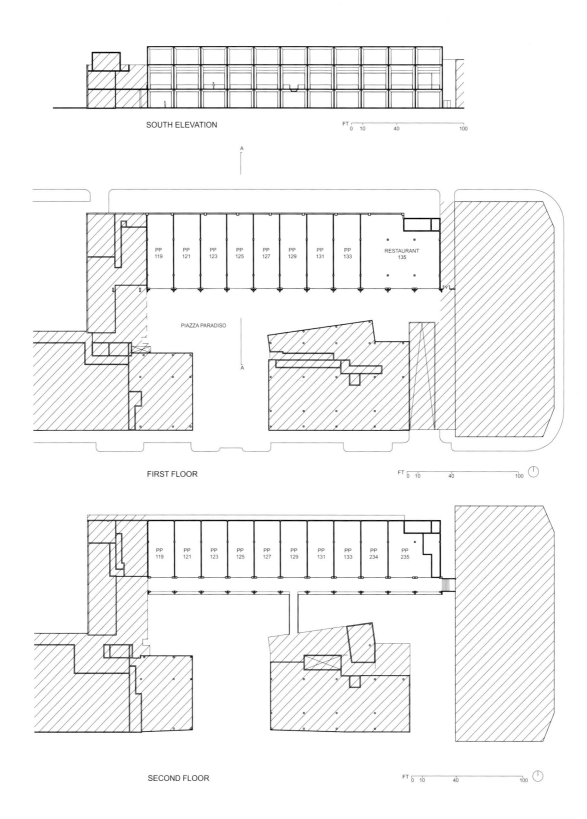

SOUTH ELEVATION

FT 0 10   40   100

A

PP   PP   PP   PP   PP   PP   PP   PP   RESTAURANT
119   121   123   125   127   129   131   133   135

PIAZZA PARADISO

A

FIRST FLOOR

FT 0 10   40   100

PP   PP   PP   PP   PP   PP   PP   PP   PP   PP
119   121   123   125   127   129   131   133   234   235

SECOND FLOOR

FT 0 10   40   100

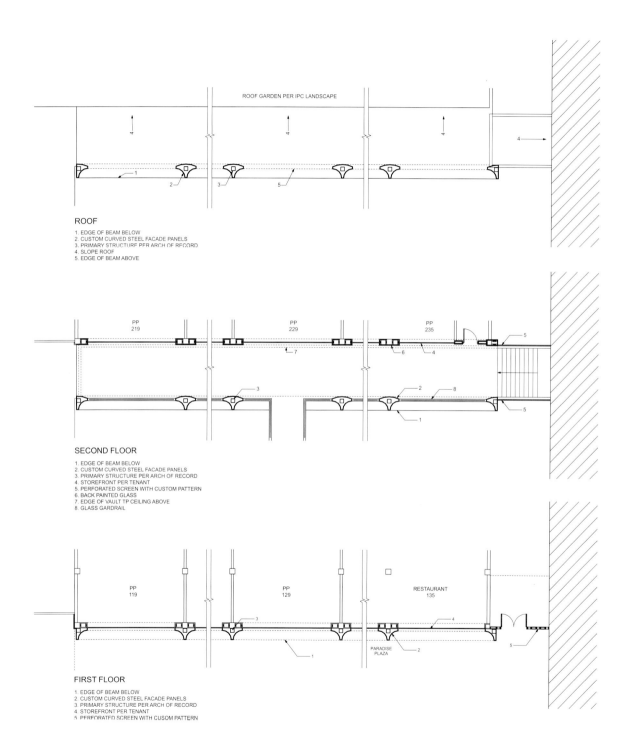

ROOF GARDEN PER IPC LANDSCAPE

ROOF

1. EDGE OF BEAM BELOW
2. CUSTOM CURVED STEEL FACADE PANELS
3. PRIMARY STRUCTURE PER ARCH OF RECORD
4. SLOPE ROOF
5. EDGE OF BEAM ABOVE

PP
219

PP
229

PP
235

SECOND FLOOR

1. EDGE OF BEAM BELOW
2. CUSTOM CURVED STEEL FACADE PANELS
3. PRIMARY STRUCTURE PER ARCH OF RECORD
4. STOREFRONT PER TENANT
5. PERFORATED SCREEN WITH CUSTOM PATTERN
6. BACK PAINTED GLASS
7. EDGE OF VAULT TP CEILING ABOVE
8. GLASS GARDRAIL

PP
119

PP
129

RESTAURANT
135

PARADISE
PLAZA

FIRST FLOOR

1. EDGE OF BEAM BELOW
2. CUSTOM CURVED STEEL FACADE PANELS
3. PRIMARY STRUCTURE PER ARCH OF RECORD
4. STOREFRONT PER TENANT
5. PERFORATED SCREEN WITH CUSOM PATTERN

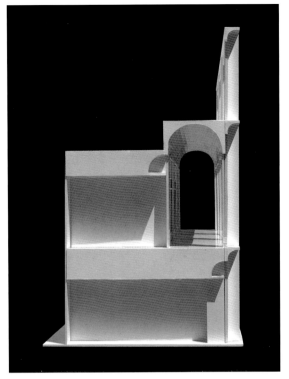

Model section detail

Interior view of covered arcade

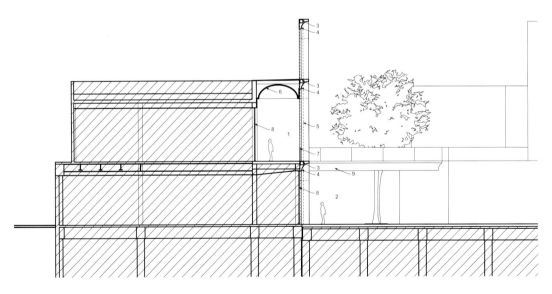

FIRST FLOOR

1. COVERED ARCADE
2. PIAZZA PARADISO
3. STRL. SUPPORT FOR FACADE PANELS
4. CURVED STEEL FACADE PANEL BEAM COVER
5. CURRVED STEEL FACADE COLUMN BEYOND
6. VAULTED STUCCO CEILING
7. GLASS GARDRAIL
8. STOREFRONT PER TENANT
9. BRIDGE BEYOND

HOME VALUES

Johnston Marklee's Sale House, the National Psyche, and the Rise and Fall of "Flipper" Gray

ASHLEY BIGHAM

A Sunday afternoon spent strolling through open houses in middle America will leave one feeling, well, a bit gray. Not dull or gloomy, but enveloped in the cozy comfort of velvety gray paint. Scroll for a few minutes through Zillow, the nation's leading real estate app, and you'll see the same thing: the domestic beige, cream, and cotton-colored walls of the 1990s have been replaced by light gray, silver, and slate as America's favorite home values. Turn on any of the surfeit of HGTV remodeling shows that have aired in the decade since the 2008 housing crisis and it is abundantly clear: kitchen walls, bathroom walls, and living room walls, all feature nearly identical palettes of gray, the unofficial national signifier that a house has been renovated or "flipped"' and is ready for market.

Why gray? The market offers one answer: gray adds value. Johnston Marklee's Sale House, completed in 2004 before the gray trend kicked off, offers another: because it makes the world seem more—or less—real.

Gray's value proposition in the real estate context is its assumed neutrality. But gray is not without distinction. Gray can be warm or cool. It can have undertones of violet, blue, or green. Behr's *Dolphin Fin* and Benjamin Moore's *Gray Owl* remind us that grays found in nature are textured: wet and slick, or soft and downy. Sherwin-Williams's *Light French Gray* with its purple undertones and stormy cool hue can seem exotic or historic depending on the context. Benjamin Moore's *Balboa Mist* isolates, like drifting into an unknown sea. Choosing between Sherwin-Williams's *Agreeable Gray*, *Mindful Gray*, or *Repose Gray* suggests that gray is not a color, but a state of mind. It allows viewers to imagine their interior spaces as blank canvases ready to accept a new identity—and all the possibilities that entails. At the Sale House, it is the *exterior* of the house that receives this treatment while the interiors alternate between white and bright pops of turquoise, amber, and pink.

When Johnston Marklee collaborated with artist Jeff Elrod on the exterior paint of the Sale House, Elrod suggested the house be painted the value of a 'gray card.' A gray card is a technical tool used to calibrate image exposure and color in photographs or

Sale House

Sale House courtyard

video. It uses a value known as 'middle gray'—a standard neutral tone perceptually halfway between white and black—to bring out the highest saturation of other colors. Used in this technical way by photographers, gray becomes a homing device for the entire color spectrum. It is a frame for viewing the world, an absolute that spans digital and analog methods of image production.

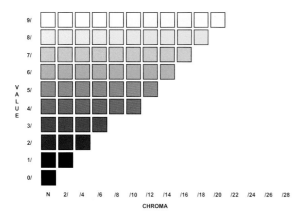

Reproduction of Munsell's chroma chart

In color theory, *value* describes the lightness of a color, often understood on a scale of one to ten, where zero is pure black and ten is pure white. In the 1929 *Munsell Book of Color*, color theorist Albert H. Munsell uses a 'pure' gray scale to measure each color in the spectrum and assign it a 'home value'—the point on the scale at which a color hue reaches its maximum chroma effect. For example, yellow is most intense at a light value (a gray value of 9), while violet is strongest at a dark value (a gray value of 4 or 5). Since pure gray is a neutral color made of only black and white with no chroma, *it has no home value.* The lack of value that makes the world pop in Staudenmaier's photos and creates ambiguity in the photographs of Livia Corona Benjamin is intrinsic to the core concept of gray. It is the ultimate expression and purpose of the neutral tone.

As seen in photos of the Sale House by Eric Staudenmaier, this most neutral of tones registers the full value of the adjacent colors—the sky is lighter than the house, the surrounding fence darker, the asphalt shingles a near definite match. The gray facade kisses the asphalt shingle roof of the adjacent house, disappearing into its ordinariness. At night the house appears almost black, dissolving into the night sky. Reflections from the interior walls create vibrant glows of pink and blue.

Conceptually, that neutrality of gray manifests very differently in the photographs of Livia Corona Benjamin, an artist who collaborated with Johnston Marklee to create staged photographs of the house using actors, costumes, and props. In one of her photos, an elderly couple wearing gray suits stare at the Sale House, a small, red "FOR SALE" sign perched on the balcony. The photo conveys the trepidation of house-hunting: the hesitation of the prospective buyers or potential sellers, the uncertainty of momentous decisions and new beginnings. But its meaning is unclear. Is the couple moving in or out of the house? Is this a beginning or end? What possibilities do they see in its grayness?

We can't possibly know and that's the point. These photos go beyond documentation and create a layered and curious domestic narrative, a rich architectural and social experience that acknowledges the life of a house. It's no surprise that the iconic value stands in for multiple metaphors in this series: gray hair, gray suits, gray days, gray matter, gray noise, gray years, gray area. Gray is a state of being which is ambiguous and unknowable. In these photos, gray is no longer a frame for viewing a spectrum of colors; grayness is both the subject and the quality of the image. It's hard to assign it any value at all.

From a color theory perspective, it's ironic that the value-less gray became the flipper's favorite. And in many ways, it's fitting that one of Pantone's 2021 Colors of the Year was *Ultimate Gray*, a cool if somewhat generic tone meant to "encourage feelings of composure, steadiness, and resilience." *Ultimate Gray.* The name is perhaps more apt than intended, as it seems to be marking the end of the color's dominance in popular culture. All trends come to an end, and even gray is not immune to oversaturation, regardless of its perceived value. Looking back at the last decade of interior grays, maybe we missed an opportunity to demand something more than the calm reassurance of *Ultimate Gray.* Maybe we missed a chance to leverage gray's unknowability to question our surroundings, to question our future goals, our aspirations as a nation, *our* values. Instead of looking critically at our surroundings, we chose to paint over what was there to make life feel fresh and new, to erase disruptions or anomalies. Doing this, we were told, would put our minds at ease and increase our home value.

Now, as we move from one housing crisis to another in America (from the foreclosure crisis of 2008 to the affordable housing crisis of today), the Sale House shows us the true missed potential of the "flipper" gray. Where we once saw gray as a blank slate and the quickest route to architecture's monetization, the Sale House—and Albert H. Munsell—shows us how gray can be both a useful tool and an independent subject. The obsession with domestic consumption and real estate investment obscured the simple fact that the value of a home is much more than monetary. The Sale House shows us what could have been. It asks us to pause and consider, to use architecture as a tool for truly seeing the world, and also as a world unto itself—complete and fulfilled.

Sale House, 18% Grey by Livia Corona Benjamin

PROJECT CREDITS & DATA

Menil Drawing Institute (2012-2018)

Client: The Menil Collection

Location: Houston, Texas

Status: Completed

Architecture Team: Sharon Johnston, Mark Lee, Nicholas Hofstede, Andri Luescher, Anton Schneider, Rodolfo Reis Dias, Jeff Mikolajewski, Maria Letizia Garzoli, Douglas Harsevoort, Elizabeth Jones, Maximilian Kocademirci, David Gray, Mehr Kanpour, Mike Todd, Toni-Maria Anschuetz
Collaborators: Gilbane (contractor), MVVA (landscape), Guy Nordenson and Associates (structure), Cardno Haynes Whaley (associate structure), Stantec (MEP), Lockwood Andrews Newnam (civil), Simpson Gumpertz & Heger (building enclosure), George Sexton Associates (lighting), Tillett (landscape lighting), AECOM (cost estimating), Arup (acoustic & AV/IT), Architect's Security Group (security), ACI (code), Terracon (geotech), Olsson (soils), WC3 (irrigation)

UCLA Margo Leavin Graduate Art Studios (2016-2019)

Client: University of California Los Angeles

Location: Culver City, CA, USA

Status: Completed

Architecture Team: Sharon Johnston, Mark Lee, Nicholas Hofstede, Lindsay Erickson, Tori McKenna, David Gray, Ryan Hernandez
Collaborators: UCLA Capital Programs (project management), Abbott Construction (contractor), Simpson Gumpertz & Heger (structure & building envelope), Pamela Burton & Company (landscape), KPFF (civil), ME Engineers (MEP), Horton Lees Brogden (lighting), Veneklasen (acoustics & AV/IT), Jensen Hughes (code & accessibility), Van Duesen Associates (vertical transportation), C Plus C Consulting (specifications), Mollet Geiser & Co (environmental graphics), Capital Projects Group (cost estimating), GAIA (LEED), Places Studio (visualizations)

UIC Center for the Arts (2018-2019)

Client: University of Illinois at Chicago

Location: Harrison Field, Chicago, Illinois

Status: Competition

Architecture Team: Sharon Johnston, Mark Lee, Nicholas Hofstede, Anton Schneider, Justin Kim, Miaojie Ted Zhang, Elena Hasbun, Alicia Chen, Isabel Strauss, Seunghyun Kang
Collaborators: UrbanWorks (AOR), LERA (structure), BuroHappold (MEP), Reed Hilderbrand (landscape), Schuler Shook (theatre), Threshold (acoustics & AV/IT), TERRA (civil), Thirst (environmental graphics), CCS (cost estimating), 1825 (visualization)

Museum of Contemporary Art Chicago (2015-2017)

Client: Museum of Contemporary Art Chicago

Location: Chicago, Illinois

Status: Completed

Architecture Team: Sharon Johnston, Mark Lee, Nicholas Hofstede, Lindsay Erickson, Jeff Mikolajewski, Juan Salazar, Nathan Kiebler, Ellen Marsh
Collaborators: Harley Ellis Devereaux (AOR), Simpson Gumpertz & Heger (structure), Environmental Systems Design (MEP), George Sexton Associates (lighting), Cerami (AV/IT), Kirkegaard (acoustics), Lerch Bates (vertical transport), Places Studio (visualization), 1825 (visualization)

Casa de Mont (2014-2020)

Location: Pacific Palisades, Los Angeles, California

Status: Completed

Architecture Team: Sharon Johnston, Mark Lee, Rodolfo Reis Dias, Anton Schneider, Mary Casper, Jeff Mikolajewski, Fiona Cuypersstanienda, Nathan Kiebler, David Himelman
Collaborators: RJC Builders (contractor), William Koh & Associates (structure), Meline Engineering (MEP), C.W. Howe (civil), Loisos Ubbelohde (lighting), Pamela Burton & Company (landscape), Studio Shamshiri (interiors)

Porch House (2011-2013)

Location: Los Angeles, CA

Status: Completed

Architecture Team: Sharon Johnston, Mark Lee, Anton Schneider, Katrin Terstegen, Lindsay Erickson, Gary Ku, Ian Thomas, Mie Benson, Philipp Breuer
Collaborators: Simpson Gumpertz & Heger (structure), Antieri & Haloossim Consulting Engineers (MEP & FPE), Greenlee & Associates (landscape), Luminesce Design Inc. (lighting), C.W. Howe Partners Inc. (civil), Geosystems, Inc. (geotechnical), Loisos + Ubbelohde (sustainability), Rob Southern (interior design), Bulthaup (kitchen design), Pacific Crest Consultants (expeditor), Becker & Miyamoto (surveyor); RJC Builders, Inc.(contractor)

IMAGE CREDITS

Hut House (2010-2014)

Client: Chan Luu

Location: Kauai, Hawaii

Status: Completed

Architecture Team: Sharon Johnston, Mark Lee, Nicholas Hofstede, Andri Luescher, Lindsay Erickson, Anton Schneider, Allessandro Carrea, Karl Wruck, David Gray

Collaborators: Roy K. Yamamoto & Associates (AOR), Project Design Inc (structure), Esaki Engineers (civil), KMT II (geotech), Luniesce Design (lighting), GSLA Studio (landscape), Aqua Engineers (septic), 360 Site (survey), Island Solar (solar)

Philadelphia Contemporary (2018-2019)

Client: Philadelphia Contemporary

Location: Philadelphia, PA, US

Status: Concept Design

Architecture Team: Sharon Johnston, Mark Lee, Andri Luescher, Lindsay Erickson, Seunghyun Kang, Ryan Hernandez, Toshiki Nimi, Miaojie Ted Zhang

Collaborators: MGA (AOR), LERA Consulting Engineers (structure), Vanderweil (MEP), Meliora (civil), Andropogon (landscape), Transsolar (climate engineering), Mollet Geiser & Co (environmental graphics), Tillotson (lighting), Directional Logic (cost estimating), 1825 (visualization)

Miami Design District (2012-2017)

Client: Dacra

Location: Miami, FL, US

Status: Completed

Architecture Team: Sharon Johnston, Mark Lee Lindsay Erickson, Rodolfo Reis Dias, Thibaut Pierron, Austin Kaa

Collaborators: SB Architects (associate architect), Duany Plater-Zyberk (master plan architects), CHM Engineering (structural), TLC Engineering (MEP), Island Planning Corporation (landscape), Spiers & Major (lighting)

All reasonable efforts have been made to trace the copyright holders of the visual material reproduced in this book. The publisher and the Knowlton School apologize to anyone who has not been reached. Errors and omissions should be brought to our attention and will be corrected in future editions. All images and drawings courtesy of Johnston Marklee, except as follows:

Courtesy of Johnston Marklee. Visualization by 1825: 15 (top and bottom), 35, 75 (top and middle), 77 (both), 78, 79 (both), 93 (both), 142 (all)

Photos by Eric Staudenmaier: 8 (left), 9 (top), 10 (top), 12 (bottom), 13 (all), 14 (all), 21, 25, 29, 30, 109 (both), 119 (bottom), 124 (both), 125 (top left), 126 (top right), 129 (bottom), 134 (both), 137 (top), 140, 141 (top), 157 (both)

Photo by Gustavo Frittegotto: 10 (bottom)

Photos by Carlos Domenech: 15 (middle), 151 (bottom right), 153, 156 (top right)

Photos by Louis Heilbronn: 16 (both), 44, 45

Courtesy of Johnston Marklee. Visualization by Places Studio: 17 (top), 94 (top and bottom right), 95 (bottom), 97 (top)

Courtesy of the Menil Collection. Photos by Richard Barnes: 17 (bottom), 18, 19 (both), 42 (bottom), 52 (top and bottom left), 53 (bottom right), 57 (both), 59 (bottom), 61 (top left), 63 (top)

Courtesy of the Menil Collection. Photo by Paul Hester: 59 (top)

Courtesy of Johnston Marklee. Visualization by Igor Brozyna: 39 (bottom), 69 (top)

Photo by Phil Arnold: 49

Photos by Iwan Baan: 69 (bottom), 71 (both)

Courtesy of MCA Chicago. Photos by Kendal McCaughtery + Hall & Merrick: 102 (top left and top right)

Photo by Livia Corona Benjamin: 159

BIOGRAPHIES

BENJAMIN WILKE is the editor of the *Source Books in Architecture* series. He teaches design studios and other courses in architecture at the Knowlton School at The Ohio State Univeristy. He has edited publications on the work of Stan Allen, Preston Scott Cohen, Neil Denari, Ryue Nishizawa / SANAA, and Rem Koolhaas / OMA AMO.

SHARON JOHNSTON is Professor in Practice at the Harvard Graduate School of Design; she has taught at Princeton University and the University of California, Los Angeles and has held the Cullinan Chair at Rice University and the Frank Gehry International Chair at the University of Toronto. In 2019, Sharon Johnston was named Architectural Record's *Women in Architecture: New Generation Leader*.

MARK LEE is the Chair of the Department of Architecture at the Harvard Graduate School of Design. He has also taught at Princeton University, the University of California, Los Angeles, the Technical University of Berlin, and ETH Zurich. He has held the Cullinan Chair at Rice University and the Frank Gehry International Chair at the University of Toronto.

ASHLEY BIGHAM is co-director of Outpost Office and an Assistant Professor at the Knowlton School at The Ohio State University. She has been a Fulbright Fellow in Ukraine, a MacDowell Fellow, and a Walter B. Sanders Fellow at the University of Michigan's Taubman College of Architecture and Urban Planning. Her writing and work has appeared in publications such as *MAS Context*, *Metropolis*, *Mark*, *CLOG*, and *Surface*. The design work of Outpost Office has been exhibited at the Chicago Architecture Biennial, the Milwaukee Art Museum, the Tallinn Architecture Biennale, Roca London Gallery, Wedge Gallery, and The Cooper Union.

TODD GANNON is a professor of architecture at the Knowlton School at The Ohio State University. His books include *Reyner Banham and the Paradoxes of High Tech*, *The Light Construction Reader*, *Et in Suburbia Ego: José Oubrerie's Miller House*, *A Confederacy of Heretics* (with Ewan Branda), and monographs on the work of Morphosis, Bernard Tschumi, UN Studio, Steven Holl, Mack Scogin Merrill Elam Architects, Peter Eisenman, and Eric Owen Moss.

ACKNOWLEDGMENTS

I would like to extend a big thank you to all of those who helped make this publication possible. I am especially grateful to Sharon Johnston and Mark Lee for their generosity. Thanks to everyone at Johnston Marklee. Nichole Valliere deserves a special thanks, as her communication and effort with all things related to this publication was essential at every step.

Thank you to Ashley Bigham and Todd Gannon, whose contributions to the content included here provide original perspectives on the work of Johnston Marklee. At the Knowlton School, Dorothee Imbert and Todd Gannon have been and continue to be incredibly generous in their support of the *Source Books in Architecture* series. Thank you to Jaimie Mollison, Carla Sharon, and the whole of the Knowlton School administrative team for their assistance with this and every publication.

A continued thanks to Gordon Goff and Jake Anderson at ORO/AR+D for their guidance, expertise, and patience.

Finally, Brittney Wilson's assistance has been critical to the success of this project. Her constant attention to detail has been invaluable. Thank you.